SOLDIERS, SCHOLARS, AND SOCIETY

The Social Impact of the American Military

SOLDIERS, SCHOLARS, AND SOCIETY

The Social Impact of the American Military

EDWARD BERNARD GLICK
Temple University

GOODYEAR PUBLISHING COMPANY, INC.
Pacific Palisades, California

©1971 by
Edward Bernard Glick

Library of Congress Catalog Card Number: 74-144839

ISBN: 0-87620-873-1 (P)   Y-8731-5
        0-87620-874-X (C)   Y-874X-1

Current printing (last number):
10 9 8 7 6 5 4 3 2 1

Printed in the United States of America

To my parents, Louis and Ray Glick

Where there is much desire to learn, there of necessity will be much arguing, much writing, many opinions; for opinion in good men is but knowledge in the making.

John Milton, *Areopagitica* (1644)

Contents

List of Figures

List of Tables

Acknowledgments

This book would never have come about without the encouraging help of many people. I have in mind in particular my publisher, Al Goodyear; my production editor, Barry Weissman; the Trustees of Temple University, Dean George W. Johnson of its College of Liberal Arts, and Professor Harry A. Bailey, Jr., chairman of its political science department, for awarding me research grants in 1968 and 1969; my Temple colleagues, Professors Daniel J. Elazar, Gerard J. Mangone, Benjamin Schoenfeld, and Murray S. Stedman, Jr., L. Howard Bennett, the Defense Department's Director for Civil Rights; I. M. Greenberg and Frank M. McKernan, the respective Directors of the Defense Department's Projects 100,000 and Transition; the publishers of *Air Force Space Digest, Foreign Service Journal, Military Review*, and *P.S.*, the newsletter of the American Political Science Association, for letting me use material I first published in their pages; my research assistants, A. John Berrigan, Edward J. Laurence, Jay Shafritz, and Richard Smith; my typists, Miss Linda Scherr, Mrs. Doris Shinn, and Mrs. Harriet Schulman; my wife, Florence, and my children, Reuven and Marnina, for learning how to live with a hot-tempered author; and Lawrence P. Greenberg of Havertown, Pennsylvania, for being a good friend and critic.

But while I am very grateful to all of these people, I am most grateful to my students.

1

For Those
Who Skip Prefaces

Like all books, this one is the joint product of style, method, fact, and interpretation. My dictionary defines a fact as "that which actually exists," as "reality," as "a truth known by actual experience or observation." But is there really such a thing as an uninterpreted fact, uninfluenced by the person who is experiencing or observing it?

Take chemistry or physics, for instance. Two students are in a laboratory looking at half a glass of water. Their instructor asks them what they see. The first says he sees a glass of water that is half full; the second, one that is half empty. They are both right, of course, for both are describing a real and true fact, which they are observing simultaneously. Yet how differently they each perceive and interpret that fact.

If this is a problem when one deals with the more exact disciplines such as physics and chemistry and with so clear and incontrovertible a "fact" as a glass of water, how much more is it so when the discipline is one of the social sciences and the subject is the military, neither of which is very exact or without controversy?

As for my approach to method and style, one can best understand it within the context of the Great Debate that is bogging down political science today. The argument is between the Traditionalists and the Behavioralists. When you ask the first what they usually mean by the second they talk pejoratively about the "methodologists," "quanti-fiers," and "numerologists," who are more concerned with the methods of science than the substance of politics. When you ask the second about their perceptions of the first, they usually talk, also somewhat derisively, about the "philosophers," "narrativists," and "journalists," who subjectively intuit when they should be engaging in objective scientific method.

Interestingly, this kind of argument doesn't occur very often among physical and biological scientists. Being in older, more estab-lished, more appreciated, and more objective disciplines, they have no identity crises. They *know* they are scientists and they know the public knows it too. So they do not have to reassure themselves con-stantly or to prove to others that this is so. They are therefore much less critical of intuition and much more sceptical of "The Scientific Method" than their colleagues in the social sciences. Louis I. Kuslan and A. Harris Stone, in their excellent book *Teaching Children Science: An Inquiry Approach*, recall the oft-quoted statement of the late Nobel laureate in physics, Percy Williams Bridgeman, that "the scientific method, as far as it is a method, is nothing more than doing one's damnedest with one's mind, no holds barred." And they note that a top-notch scientist will often acknowledge "the role of intuition, hunch, chance thought, and the lucky accident in his research. Charles Nicolle, who first recognized how typhus was spread, wrote about this 'sudden flash of creative illumination. . . . This shock, this sudden illumination, this instantaneous self-certainty of a new fact—I know of it, I have experienced it in my own life.' "[1]

The great pity in the dichotomous and divisive debate in political science is that it is so wasteful of time and energy. More than that, it is futile and false. In *all* social scholarship (not just political science) there is room and need for some to ask questions, others to unearth facts, for some to rely on good history, thinking, and insight, others to work on all forms of method—and for all of us to write well.

If the study of politics means anything, it means the study of people relating to power. You cannot study politics without being interested in the kinds of behavior that tell us something about how and why people do political things or have political things done to them. But you can be interested in political behavior without relying mainly on numbers and lines in place of words. Every political scientist worth his salt is at least a qualitative behavioralist. Thus the word "behavioral" ought not to be used as a synonym for "quantitative" or "methodological."

---

1. Louis I. Kuslan and A. Harris Stone, *Teaching Children Science: An Inquiry Ap-proach* (Belmont, California: Wadsworth Publishing Company, Inc., 1968), pp. 15–18.

A sociologist who read this book while it was still in manuscript recognized that my main purpose is to discuss some very live policy issues in a very lively way. But he also labeled it "atheoretical" and methodologically "nonrigorous." He was right.

The fact is that I am simply *not* a quantifying methodologist or a theoretically oriented political scientist. Issues and viewpoints, not methodologies and theories, are what now concern my students and I. I have used theories and published quantified data and models, but I neither worship nor depend upon them exclusively. I respect theory and quantification and the credentials and motives of those who use them, but so do I respect insight and intuition and those scholars who have these qualities. Good intuition is always superior to bad—or badly interpreted—data. Like all scholars, I want to be precise and I want to be right. But if I must choose between precision and truth, I would rather be imprecisely right than precisely wrong.

By the standards of the narrow definition of Behavioralism which, as it relates to political science, should really be called *polimetrics*, I use no method at all. For my method is to hypothesize and then to read, think, and talk to people in several successive cycles until I am ready to write—and rewrite. And when I write, I try desperately not to write in social scientific jargon: that code-language that often hides more than it reveals and that even recognized specialists in a field cannot always understand. Instead, I cling stubbornly to the conviction that a social scholar loses neither his membership in the Footnote Fraternity nor his scientific manhood if he chooses to write in the language of the interested layman.

2

The American Military: Can Anything "Bad" Ever Really Be "Good"?*

I teach a course in the politics of national defense. Besides the usual stress on the relationship between military and foreign policies, I regularly cover the moral, philosophical, psychological, and domestic economic and social implications generated by the existence of armies and their possible and actual use.

During one of the sessions, a student began the following dialogue with me:

STUDENT. I am against the war in Vietnam because I am a pacifist.

TEACHER. Fine, a pacifist is one who believes that force, even so-called legal force, is never justified, and pacifism is an ancient doctrine respected by many who oppose it. But may I ask you a few questions? Did you favor President Johnson's sending of Marines into the Dominican Republic?

STUDENT. Of course not. I just told you that I am a pacifist. I couldn't support it regardless of the political issues involved.

TEACHER. I wasn't in favor of it either, even though I am not a pacifist. Now I know that you are a strong civil libertarian and are opposed to the racial discrimination practiced by the white leaders of South Africa. Is that right?

*Reprinted with permission from *Air Force/Space Digest*, official journal of the Air Force Association, 1750 Pennsylvania Avenue, N.W., Washington, D.C. 20006.

STUDENT. Very much so. I believe that the present racist regime in South Africa is among the most abominable in the entire world.

TEACHER. So do I, and I'm not a pacifist. Now answer this question for me quickly, if you will. Would you favor President Johnson's issuing an ultimatum to South Africa which said that if *apartheid* were not immediately lifted and if the whites there did not seriously begin to give the blacks all the democratic rights of government that their sheer numbers entitle them to, the United States would in the name of elementary humanity and justice send the Marines into South Africa?

STUDENT. Yes, I—

TEACHER. Now hold on. Whatever else you want to say, you are not a pacifist. At the most, you're a kind of "selective pacifist." Essentially, whether or not you realize it, you believe in the doctrine of the just war, and you want to be able to make up your own mind as to when and whether a particular military action is just or unjust. If you think about it for awhile, you will realize that many nonpacifists struggle with this same problem whether it be in Vietnam, the Dominican Republic, South Africa, or elsewhere.

I do not know whether I convinced my student.

If you have no army and don't need one, you have no problem. If you are a real pacifist, who sincerely believes in and is working for the immediate abolition of all armies everywhere, you have a problem, but one that *seems* easy to handle conceptually and morally. I say *seems* easy because if a man wears a uniform, is trained in the use of weapons, and is under society's discipline, in practical terms it often makes little difference that you call him a soldier, a reservist, a militiaman, a national guardsman, or a policeman. If you are a true pacifist, you can simply argue that if only society would eliminate all of its war planners, war fighters, and war material producers, you would be rid not only of the military-industrial complex's influence on foreign and defense policies, but on all other domestic public policies as well.

But what if, however reluctantly, you honestly believe that at least for a while longer in this world even a democracy must possess warriors, weapons, and weapons makers? In that case, you do have a problem. It is a very real one with very real and complicated conceptual, moral, political, and administrative overtones. For what you are dealing with then is not the abolition of an institution and its pervasive influences. Instead, you must struggle to understand it sufficiently so that you may control, regulate, and use both its anticipated and unanticipated influences for the greatest possible public good.

This is frankly not easy to do. For one thing, there is the subjectivity-objectivity spectrum. Obviously, too much subjectivity is not good. It closes the mind, forcing it into only one or two predetermined, programmed directions. Yet, despite what many scientists and scholars say, too much objectivity is also bad because, as Sally Carrighar remarked in her wonderful book on animal behavior, only "a certain amount of subjective interest can call intuition into play, and intuition can furnish leads to more understanding."[1] Moreover, all of us—scientists and scholars are the least able or willing to admit this—are the products of our backgrounds. We are all the prisoners of our perceptions of the past and the present, and of our hopes for the future. Nowhere is this truer than in discussions of the military institution in contemporary America, especially as we try to work our way out of the trauma of the Vietnam War.

Consider: in universities and other centers of intellect a sociologist, social psychologist, or psychiatrist who studies crime is usually called a criminologist; he is never called a criminal. Similarly, a lawyer who choses to practice criminal rather than civil law is called a criminal lawyer and not a criminal. Certainly no one dares to suggest that the longer criminologists study crime or criminal lawyers defend criminals, the greater will be the likelihood that they will absorb the attributes of the people they study or defend. And no one says that they want lots of crime so that they can get more contracts, consultations, and clients.

Yet the same social critic who can remain rather unemotional about criminologists, criminal lawyers, crime, and even criminals, often quickly exhibits great emotional bias against the military practitioner. Even more quickly does he transfer that bias from the military institution and those inside it to scholars on the outside who are studying and trying to fathom it. I reject this notion. The conventional campus wisdom to the contrary, studying the military or even consulting for it under the proper conditions of academic freedom and disclosure does not automatically make you a Dr. Strangelove.

A good example of illogical antimilitarism was provided by Professor Kenneth E. Boulding of the University of Colorado. During a defense debate at Duke some years ago, he said to Harvard's Thomas C. Schelling: "I am so frightened by the intellectual renaissance of the military. . . . The thing that frightens me about intellectual people is that they believe their abstractions."[2] If this is true, why single out the military intellectual for special condemnation? And was Boulding

---

1. Sally Carrighar, *Wild Heritage* (Boston: Houghton Mifflin, 1965), p. 105.
2. Duke University Symposium Committee, *Dimensions of Defense*, Symposium held on 11 to 14 November 1962 (Durham, North Carolina, 1962), pp. 79–80.

implying that he would be less frightened by a renaissance of military mediocrity or even stupidity? Did he mean that a stupid staff officer is to be preferred to a smart one and is less dangerous to society than a smart one? The late Elmer Davis commented on this relationship between thinking and policy when he said on one of his broadcasts that if bad thinking led to bad policy, the only cure is *more* thinking. Hopefully, it will lead to good policy.

Stupid or smart, the military under our form of government has the constitutional *duty* to give the president and Congress military advice. From an overall viewpoint, that advice can often be very bad advice, but the military cannot *make* them take it. On Vietnam, for example, I seriously doubt that Presidents Kennedy, Johnson, and Nixon took any military advice they did not really want to take, nor do I think that Congress as a whole made military appropriations it did not want to make. Our military involvement there could have ended whenever Congress had the will or courage to stop supplying money for it. Congress has been "using" the military at least as much as the military has been "using" Congress.

What is badly needed is more political relativity, which most professors of comparative politics and American government do not apparently teach. In studying any political institution—above all, the military—one must always ask at least these questions: What are the country's problems compared to other countries' problems? How does the institution compare with its predecessors and with its contemporary counterparts elsewhere? Compared to others, how does it perform its roles, given the realities, requirements, and responsibilities that face it? How, again relative to others, can it be changed and reformed, when this is necessary, and how rapidly can such changes and reforms be made? When it interacts with other units of government and society, is it alone always and completely responsible for the ground rules under which such interactions occur, and for the results that stem from them? If, for example, it happens that in some areas of scholarly social and political research the Department of Defense is our version of the Soviet Academy of Sciences, is this necessarily because of militaristic empire-building, or because Congress, in its sovereign niggardliness and narrowness, has chosen to deny to the State Department, the United States Information Agency, or the Agency for International Development the authority and necessary funds to do or contract out such research for themselves?

Only political relativity provides the proper perspective for answering such questions and for making a fair appraisal of the American military's domestic impact, as well as of the impact of events and other domestic institutions upon the American military. Only political relativity brings home the true significance of the posture of the American army as compared to, let us say, the army of France. Unlike General Charles de Gaulle, who ruled in what is also a democracy, no American president has ever faced an armed revolt by his colonels and generals, and after putting the revolt down, pardoned most of the insurrectionists anyway. Unlike De Gaulle, no American president has felt compelled to fly to a secret midnight rendezvous with leading military commanders in order to secure in advance their support and that of their units for impending political battles in which he is about to engage in the domestic arena. Certainly no American president fears a military confrontation with his commanders if he adopts internal or external policies they cannot approve of. The American military simply does not surround the White House, the Senate, the House of Representatives, the State legislatures, and the county courthouses and announce. "You have five minutes to turn over the reins of government to us, or else!"

The effectiveness of our political "fail-safe" system does not lie in the fact that the commander of a loaded Strategic Air Command bomber is physically or technically unable to fly over Washington and threaten its destruction if the civilian government refuses to resign. It lies rather in the fact that such an act is for him simply unthinkable. And this is so, I believe, because if the professional American military man learns nothing else in the academies and other service educational institutions to which he is exposed, he learns to respect and accept the concept of civilian, that is, presidential and congressional, control of the military. Whether the President and Congress are always willing to assert and defend this concept is another question. But I am convinced that to the extent that this basic constitutional concept is being eroded by domestic men rather than by foreign events, these men are more often civilians, both in and out of Congress, who are usually, but not always, found rather far to the right of the political spectrum.

How else can one answer these questions of definition and politics? Who is the real militarist, nonmilitarist, or antimilitarist: General Eisenhower, who spent a lifetime in uniform and then warned us against the military-industrial complex, or the average senator and congressman (not just the chairmen of the armed services committees), who, though perhaps never in the army, tries to get as many military bases and contracts in his state as possible? Is the real militarist the professional military man who, in the words of Harvard's Samuel P. Huntington, "always favors preparedness, but. . . never feels prepared?" Or is it civilian politicians, civilian philosophers, civilian publicists, and even civilian academicians who have often been "the romanticizers and glorifiers of war"?[3] Isn't it probable that a bit more "militarism" (that is, actual rearmament and the willingness to use the arms) by France, Britain, and the United States in the 1930s would have stopped Hitler before World War II? And is it not at least possible that the Germans in 1938 and the Russians in 1968 would not have been tempted to rape Czechoslovakia if the Czechs and the Slovaks had projected the military stance and the mental attitude of, let us say, the present-day Yugoslavs?

For some Americans, the military is not only unmentionable, but unthinkable. But the American military will not go away. And given cold wars, hot wars, and in-between wars, when, whether, and in what fashion it should go away is highly debatable. Until it does go away, its presence will continue to be felt in the planning, decision-making, and carrying out of government policies clearly related to foreign affairs. This is well-known and accepted by most segments of our population. What is less known, or if known, less acceptable to other segments, is the role of the American military in supposedly nondefense and even nongovernmental areas that are domestic in nature.

To these segments, it makes little or no difference that this role—be it planned or unplanned, direct or indirect, expected or unexpected, or wanted or unwanted by the military itself—is often productive and positive, and sometimes progressive. In general, their reaction is that if the military conceives something positive, they must, in reflexive Pavlovian fashion, construe it as negative. For them it is an automatic given that the very existence of the military is at best a necessary evil in a disordered world and at worst an expensive and competing impediment to social progress in a disordered land.

Actually, armies have always been expensive. The real or imagined imperatives of war and diplomacy have always had to compete with the unmet domestic needs of any particular society. What appears new about this competition to the present generation of concerned people is their belief that they have suddenly discovered this truth for the very first time in history.

Since armies are expensive, and since they do draw away resources, maximizing their utility, minimizing their cost, and keeping their soldiers gainfully occupied in times of peace has always been a problem. More often than is generally realized, the solution to that problem has been directed toward nation-building and internal improvements at least as far back as the ancient Egyptians, Etruscans, Romans, and Incas.

The same thing is true for the United States. "The ax, pick, saw and trowel," Zachary Taylor wrote 150 years ago, "has become more the implement of the American soldier than the cannon, musket or

---

3. Samuel P. Huntington, *The Soldier and the State* (New York: Vintage Books, 1957), pp. 69–70

sword.''[4] While one can question his assertion that the army's nonmilitary tasks overtook its military ones, one cannot question that it did perform them often and well. The Lewis and Clark Expedition into the territory of the Louisiana Purchase, the western explorations of Lieutenant Zebulon Montgomery Pike, Captain Benjamin de Bonneville, Captain John C. Frémont, and Major Stephen H. Long, the ministering of the Medical Corps to civilians on the frontier, the medical research contributions of army doctors William Beaumont, Benjamin Waterhouse, William C. Gorgas, and Walter Reed, the introduction by West Point graduates of civil engineering into the curriculum of American universities, the Army Corps of Engineers' responsibility for internal navigation and flood control since 1816, the role of army engineering officers in early railroad construction, the War Department's management of the Depression-born camps of the Civilian Conservation Corps (the famous CCC) from 1933 to 1942, and the medical, dental, and veterinary help that army Special Forces units gave to Alaskan Indians and Eskimos in 1965—all attest to how old this tradition really is in America. It predates Soviet Russia, Communist China, our Vietnam Fixation, the political emergence of Africa and Asia, and the revolution of rightfully rising expectations by America's minority and depressed groups.

A basic question is whether, in the light of our current domestic realities, it is legitimate for our armed forces to engage in social rehabilitation. One of those who thinks so is former Secretary of Defense Robert S. McNamara, now president of the World Bank. On 7 November 1967, he began a speech to the National Association of Educational Broadcasters meeting in Denver with:

> I want to talk to you this morning about the unused potential of the Department of Defense—a potential for contributing to the solution of the social problems wracking our nation.
>
> The Defense Department is the largest single institution in the world: an institution employing directly four and a half million men and women, indirectly employing several million more, and directing the use of nearly 10 percent of the nation's wealth.
>
> The question I want to put to you is this: can these vast resources be used to contribute to our nation's benefit beyond the narrow—though vitally necessary—role of military power?[5]

He then answered his question largely in terms of the Department's own Open Housing Program, Project 100,000, and Project

---

4. Quoted in Francis Paul Prucha, *Broadax and Bayonet: The Role of the United States Army in the Development of the Northwest, 1815–1860* (Madison: State Historical Society of Wisconsin, 1953), p. 104.

5. U.S., Department of Defense, Office of the Assistant Secretary for Public Affairs. News Release No. 1061–67 (Washington, D.C., 7 November 1967), p. 1.

Transition. The Open Housing Program is an effort "to break through the barriers of racial discrimination in off-base housing for military personnel." (The pioneering efforts of the American army in trying to break down racial barriers on-base is already well-known.) Project 100,000 is a program "to salvage the poverty-scarred youth of our society at the rate of 100,000 men each year—first for two years of military service, and then for a lifetime of productive activity in civilian society." Project Transition is a program "to assist the three-quarters of a million men leaving military service each year to select and train for the role in civilian life that will contribute most to their personal fulfillment and to the nation's benefit."

Almost a year later, Clark M. Clifford, McNamara's successor until the end of the Johnson administration, made similar points in an address before the National Security Industrial Association meeting in Washington. "I do believe," he said, "that the citizens of the United States have reason to expect—and, indeed, to demand—that the element of the government which spends half of their federal tax dollars devote more of its time and more of its thinking and more of its resources to those aspects of our domestic problems which are important to our total national security."[6] He thus implied that no matter what definition of national security one used, America could never be really secure with high levels of poverty, illiteracy, unemployability, and the domestic social unrest they breed.

In the area of medical care, Secretary Clifford noted that the American Defense Department is one of the world's biggest hospital operators and users and that it wants to work with private industry in reducing the cost and raising the quality of hospital construction. He pledged military support for research in the automation of hospitals so that as much time-consuming and routinized record-keeping and laboratory and other analysis as possible could be transferred "from the overworked doctor and nurse to the sophisticated machine." He asked industry's cooperation in these efforts.

In housing, Secretary Clifford compared the average private homebuilder in the United States, who puts up less than fifty houses a year, to the Defense Department, which spends $200 million each year for new construction and an additional $450 million for maintaining and leasing present housing. The first—the private builder—lacks the resources and incentives to research and develop newer, better, and cheaper design and production techniques. The second—the Department of Defense—has both, but had done "virtually nothing" about the problem. To this end, he announced that the air force was going to use a proposed $6 million military housing program at George Air Force Base in Victorville, California to develop materials and techniques that hopefully could be passed along to the private building

6. Quoted in *New York Times*, 27 September 1968, p. 17.

sector. If successful, the program would not only reduce defense costs but might also lead to more, and more profitable, low-income housing built by private entrepreneurs. Thus, one of the civilian government agencies that will be closely watching the outcome of this project is the Department of Housing and Urban Development.

In the area of employment, Clifford mentioned that over 50 defense contractors have formal programs for training and hiring unemployables from 50 of the nation's ghettos. He urged expansion of these efforts and called for a new law which would allow a price premium for contractors willing to do their work in a way that would "relieve economic dislocation."

A problem becomes a "political" problem because it has not been solved, or is not yet solvable, at the psychological, cultural, economic, or social level. Thus, even the employment of highly skilled military retirees can move from the economic to the political arena. There are many people who are concerned about military retirees, usually officers, who after some 20 to 30 years of active duty, leave the service and become involved in certain civilian pursuits. Given the frequency with which these pursuits take the form of employment with the Defense Department, the latter's so-called "think tanks," other government departments, and especially defense contractors, it is neither surprising nor wrong that people should be unhappy.

But what *should* you do with a military retiree who obviously cannot escape or undo his military background. Should you prevent him from working at all after retirement, forcing him to live only on his pension? Should you severely restrict his postmilitary choices of gainful employment? If you do restrict the choices, what should they be? Should you let him retire at 100 percent of his highest base pay (as is done in some countries) with the provision that he may not work at anything else for money? And if you adopt this alternative, will this not raise the military budget even more and deprive society of his productivity and experience in his remaining employable years? Or should you straddle the whole problem by not letting any career servicemen retire before 65? If you do this, then aren't you really opting for an all-professional army, with thousands of men who will spend their entire adult life in a closed military system? Is this good? Is this the best way of protecting American society from the Prussianism that we say we fear and do not want? Merely to ask these questions is to show the interactive and elusive difficulty of the answers, answers that must not produce more problems than they solve, else they aren't answers at all.

In this same vein, one could semantically and superficially destroy the military-industrial complex almost immediately by making all private military production government operations and all private military producers government employees. But this would fool no one and solve nothing. If American society is indeed becoming militarized, there is a great deal more to its demilitarization than merely damning militarism, praying and waiting for its destruction, and playing with names and labels.

The essential fact about soldiers is that they exist. Until a time when they will not have to exist, we need more, not fewer, scholars to study objectively what soldiers do and how and why they do it. If we fail to do this, we shall leave the military free from the serious scrutiny that we apply to other segments of society. And if we so exempt the military, how can we truly allow ourselves to make critical judgements about it and still call ourselves scholars?

3

The Black Soldier

PRESIDENT [EISENHOWER] SENDS TROOPS TO LITTLE ROCK, FEDERALIZES ARKANSAS NATIONAL GUARD; TELLS NATION HE ACTED TO AVOID ANARCHY

KENNEDY FEDERALIZES MISSISSIPPI'S GUARD; MOBILIZES TROOPS, ORDERS STATE TO YIELD; ADDRESSES NATION TODAY ON RACIAL CRISIS

ALABAMA ADMITS NEGRO STUDENTS; WALLACE BOWS TO FEDERAL FORCE; KENNEDY SEES "MORAL CRISIS" IN U.S.

JOHNSON CALLS UP TROOPS, DEPLORES WALLACE'S ACTS; ALABAMA MARCH ON TODAY

21 DEAD IN LOS ANGELES RIOTS; 600 HURT; 20,000 TROOPS CALLED; PRESIDENT CONDEMNS VIOLENCE

NEWARK'S MAYOR CALLS IN GUARD AS RIOTS SPREAD

ARMY TROOPS IN CAPITAL AS NEGROES RIOT; GUARD SENT INTO CHICAGO, DETROIT, BOSTON; JOHNSON ASKS A JOINT SESSION OF CONGRESS

U.S. TROOPS SENT TO BALTIMORE; VIOLENCE EASES IN PITTSBURGH; DR. KING MOURNED IN THE NATION

These are the front-page—some of them are banner—headlines of the *New York Times* for the days following the proclaimed events.[1] Each headline says much. When grouped and viewed together, they say even more.

One of the things they say is that the same military institution that puts down black rioters in Watts, Chicago, and Newark also escorts black children and youths through lines of hate-filled whites so that they can attend integrated schools and colleges in Arkansas, Alabama, and Mississippi. One of the things the headlines do not say is that the military institution involved in runaway riot control, draft inequities, and a high black casualty rate in Vietnam is the first institution in America to have more or less desegregated itself, and one of the strongest pressure groups in the country for off-base open housing. While the military's negative roles are often and justifiably highlighted, its positive roles in domestic society are often and unjustifiably ignored.

There is more than a little irony in the history of this attitude. Take, for example, the matter of black troops in combat. During the First World War, blacks resented that they comprised one-third of the military labor force and only one-thirtieth of the combat troops.[2] After that war, in 1931, President Robert R. Moton of Tuskegee Institute complained bitterly to President Hoover that "Negro troops at Fort Benning are without arms or equipment of any sort that could be used in training for combat service." He reminded the president that Negroes

> are excellent soldiers and possessed with eager willingness in the performance of their duties under all conditions of service. It is more than unfortunate, it is an injustice, that regiments that have distinguished themselves . . . should be reduced from combat service to be menials to white regiments, without chance for training or promotion and be excluded from other branches of the services.[3]

A year before America's entry into the Second World War, Stafford King, Civilian Aide to the Secretary of War for the State of Minnesota, wrote to the War Department: "There is no physical, moral or patriotic

---

1. *New York Times,* 25 September 1957, 30 September 1962, 12 June 1963, 21 March 1965, 15 August 1965, 14 July 1967, 6 April 1968, 8 April 1968.
2. Richard J. Stillman, II, *Integration of the Negro in the U.S. Armed Forces* (New York: Frederick A. Praeger, 1968), p. 16.
3. Quoted in Ulysses Lee, *United States Army in World War II: Employment of Negro Troops* (Washington, D.C.: Office of the Chief of Military History, 1966), p. 27.

reason why the colored man, after passing the regular tests, should be denied enrollment in the regular army, the National Guard, the ROTC, or the CMTC [Citizens' Military Training Camps]."[4]

Despite the passage of time and the pleas of Moton and King, two-thirds of the almost 700,000 black men inducted during the Second World War served in segregated transportation, quartermaster, mess, and other support units. Only "2,500 saw integrated service" rather late in the war, and "many colored men were embittered by their limited opportunity for combat."[5]

After the war, when the country and the Congress debated the reintroduction of peace-time military conscription, black leaders campaigned for a draft that would give black inductees equal treatment and combat training opportunities. A. Philip Randolph, president of the Brotherhood of Sleeping Car Porters, established the Committee Against Jim Crow in Military Service and Training. Testifying before the Senate Armed Services Committee in 1948, he said: "Today I would like to make clear to this committee and through you to Congress and the American people that passage now of a Jim Crow draft may only result in mass civil disobedience." To which Wayne Morse replied: "It may well lead to indictments of treason." In the same year, Grant Reynolds, a Randolph associate, announced that "Negroes would be prepared to face prison rather than join a Jim Crow Army."[6]

What accounts for the fact that in 1948 black college students were counseling draft evasion and proclaiming "Don't Join a Jim Crow Army," while more than twenty years later the cry of many of them became "Hell, No! We Won't Go!"? Why is it that then blacks complained that the armed forces were segregated and that black men were not being given a chance to serve with dignity and fight with valor, whereas later the American military, even when integrated, became a pariah?

Mainly, it was the escalation of the increasingly unpopular Vietnam War. Specifically, it was the growing opportunity for black soldiers to engage in lethal, if unsegregated, combat. Originally conceived by both blacks and whites as a necessary step in the direction of social and psychic equality for black men, combat is now construed by many to mean unequal opportunity for the black man to be exposed to military training, military casualties, and military death. An additional psychological explanation is that, regardless of wars, the military is becoming more integrated precisely at a moment in American history when black militants are calling for more, not less, black separation from whites and from the mainstream of American society.

---

4. Ibid., p. 67.
5. Stillman, *Integration of the Negro in the U.S. Armed Forces*, p. 5.
6. Ibid., pp. 38–39.

What, then, is the statistical situation of American blacks in the American military? As of September 1968, more than 300,000 blacks were on active duty, representing nearly 9 percent of the total active forces (see Table 1). While blacks comprised a shade less than 10 percent of the total number of men in Vietnam, they made up almost 20 percent of the front-line troops. In some elite units such as the airborne or the paratroopers or the Special Forces, their number reached or exceeded 25 percent (see Table 2).[7] Black casualty rates in Vietnam have been high, higher than the percentage of blacks in the total population at home (see Table 3).

TABLE 1

Negroes in the United States
Active Armed Forces
(September 1968)

| | *(Number and Percentage)* | | |
	Officer	*Enlisted*	*Total*
Army	5,646 (3.4)	153,516 (11.4)	159,162 (10.5)
Navy	352 (0.4)	31,809 (4.8)	32,161 (4.3)
Marine Corps	196 (0.8)	32,055 (11.3)	32,251 (10.5)
Air Force	2,461 (1.8)	78,422 (10.3)	80,883 (9.0)
Total	8,655 (2.1)	295,802 (9.7)	304,457 (8.8)

Source: U.S. Department of Defense, Office of the Assistant Secretary of Defense for Manpower and Reserve Affairs, 5 February 1969.

Despite these figures, the black reenlistment rate in the army relative to whites is also high. Even when it plunged from 66.5 percent in 1966 to 31.7 percent in 1967, the rate was still higher than that of white reenlistees, which decreased from 20 percent in 1966 to 12.8 percent in 1967. In other words, even with a war that grew bigger and bloodier, one-third of the blacks as compared to one-eighth of the whites chose to reenlist.[8] Why is this so?

The answer is "rooted in economics and psychodynamics."[9] A first-time reenlistee can get a cash bonus of from $900 to $1,400. Service in the elite units brings incentive pay, such as the extra $55 a month that a paratrooper gets for jump duty. Furthermore, promotions (and accompanying pay increases) come faster for the combat duty that many black soldiers perform. For most young whites,

military careers are not considered advantageous in economic terms. However, given the Depression-like conditions under which blacks

---

7. See also *New York Times*, 29 April 1968, p. 16 and Thomas A. Johnson, "Negroes in 'the Nam' " *Ebony* 23 (August 1968), p. 33. The entire issue of this magazine is devoted to the black soldier in the American military.

8. *New York Times*, 11 July 1968, p. 9.

9. David Llorens, "Why Negroes Reenlist," *Ebony* 23 (August 1968), p. 87.

live and the fact that [military] salaries . . . have escalated along with the war in Vietnam, [to many a black man] the traditional jokes about a soldier's pay are invalid as reflections of the modern day.[10]

TABLE 2

Negro Participation in Southeast Asia
(Vietnam, Thailand, and Nearby Off-Shore Waters)

	31 December 1966 [a]		31 December 1967	
	Total	Negro (%)	Total	Negro (%)
Army	242,043	30,603 (12.6)	337,234	37,456 (11.1)
Navy	57,840	3,108 (5.4)	69,336	3,228 (4.7)
Marine Corps	67,601	5,461 (8.0)	78,374	6,462 (8.2)
Air Force	52,006	5,379 (10.3)	83,188	8,758 (10.5)
Total	419,490	44,551 (10.6)	568,132	55,904 (9.8)

	30 September 1968	
	Total	Negro (%)
Army	382,493	45,121 (11.8)
Navy	82,435	3,956 (4.8)
Marine Corps	80,164	8,554 (10.7)
Air Force	90,241	9,582 (10.6)
Total	635,333	67,213 (10.6)

[a]Excluding personnel in Thailand.
Source: U.S. Department of Defense, Office of the Assistant Secretary of Defense for Manpower and Reserve Affairs, 5 February 1969.

Psychologically, black psychiatrist Dr. Alvin F. Poussaint has explained the black soldier's voluntary association with the armed forces as follows:

Black men in general, particularly from the low socioeconomic groups and particularly from the South, suffer from a low self-esteem because of racism in American society. The black male has always been castrated by the society and has always struggled for a sense of manhood and identity in a white world. Because of the limited opportunities that a racist society allows the black man for achieving manhood, I think many young black men gravitate to the army to prove they are men by risking their lives in combat. Superior prowess in combat is one of the most primitive ways of achieving a sense of manhood. The black man in combat is ready to trade his life for psychological manhood, status and self-esteem.[11]

There is also a less combative and more civil libertarian reason for free black choice of a military career, one that can appeal to even

10. Ibid., p. 88.
11. Quoted in ibid.

highly educated black men and their wives and children. It is that, paradoxically, the military is the most integrated segment of American society. On-base, in such matters as housing, post exchanges, movies, club membership, medical care, and schooling, the equality that blacks enjoy goes far beyond what is enjoyed by their brothers and sisters in civilian America.[12] This is not to say that there are not still some serious vestiges of minority discrimination in the military—in officer promotion, for instance. However, few, if any other, visible institutions outside of the military are moving faster to eliminate such vestiges.

A case in point is Defense Department efforts to eliminate housing discrimination against servicemen and their families who live off-base.

TABLE 3

Negro Deaths by Hostile Action in Vietnam

	1961 to 1966		1967	
	Total	Negro (%)	Total	Negro (%)
Army	4,156	832 (20.0)	5,443	733 (13.5)
Navy	199	1 (0.5)	311	9 (2.9)
Marine Corps	2,027	223 (11.0)	3,452	441 (12.8)
Air Force	262	4 (1.5)	172	9 (5.2)
Total	6,644	1,060 (16.0)	9,378	1,192 (12.7)

	January through September 1968			
	Total	Negro (%)	Total	Negro (%)
Army	7,941	1,057 (13.3)	17,540	2,622 (14.9)
Navy	390	10 (2.6)	900	20 (2.2)
Marine Corps	4,055	576 (14.2)	9,534	1,240 (13.0)
Air Force	153	2 (1.3)	587	15 (2.6)
Total	12,540[a]	1,645 (13.1)	28,562	3,897 (13.6)

[a]Coast Guard, 1.

Source: U.S., Department of Defense, Office of the Assistant Secretary of Defense for Manpower and Reserve Affairs, 5 February 1969.

The average service family is moved every 2.5 to 3.5 years. By its very nature, a military family has far less choice about when and where to move than does the average civilian family. Moreover, because of congressionally imposed budget restrictions and very possibly the

12. Black Major Lavell Merritt argues a contrary view: "The American people have for years been told that the military leads the nation in breaking down and eliminating all vestiges of segregation and discriminatory treatment of minority groups. This is a blatant lie." New York Times, 14 October 1968, p. 3. What is not clear is whether the major is arguing that there are still vestiges of segregation and discrimination in the military (which is true) or that another institution outside the military surpasses it in eliminating such vestiges (which is not true).

lobbying strength of private real estate renters and developers, Defense Department policy is to construct new on-base living units only in parts of the country having the most critical housing shortages. As a result, most military families live in off-base civilian communities. From one point of view this is good. If all military families lived on military installations, their almost complete separation from civilian men, women, and children would weaken American social and political democracy. But from another point of view this is bad, for it puts military families from minority groups, especially blacks, at the mercy of local custom and prejudices in the matter of the sale and rental of suitable housing in suitable neighborhoods. And in fact, the lack of "adequate, decent off-base housing for Negro personnel in the armed forces is," says the Pentagon, "the most stubborn and pervasive form of segregation and discrimination affecting Negroes in the army, navy, marine corps and air force."[13]

This was made movingly clear by servicemen themselves, answering questionnaires about off-base housing in the Greater Washington, D.C. area:[14]

1. 15 months is the period we waited before we could get off-base housing, which was substandard. To get in, we had to sign a long-term lease, put down a large deposit, and an [sic] agree to paint the apartment in a racially segregated, rat-infested slum area. I directly attribute this period as one of the major reasons of family discord, which eventually caused a split. . . . My problem is not unique among members of my race. We're expected to perform as though these problems don't exist. It is very shattering to morale.

2. . . . local realtors with their massive congressional influence have controlled and limited the amount of military family housing in this area. The problem for the Negro servicemen is compounded by the widespread segregation practiced in the metropolitan area.

3. I have found that off-base housing is plentiful providing your origin is other than *NEGROID*. For instance, a Caucasian member of the Armed Forces whose pay status is equal to mine, can obtain housing conveniently located near his duty station (especially in this area) and in all cases will pay less rent, have all the modern facilities plus the wonderful advantage of not having to worry about his family being subjected to excessive vandalism, house breaking, rapes, mugging—you name it. The building in which I

---

13. U.S., Department of Defense, *Department of Defense Conference With Governmental Affairs Committee, National Newspaper Publishers Association, 21–22 September 1967: Resource and Reference Book* (Washington, D.C., 1967), p. 48. Cited hereafter as U.S., Department of Defense, *Resource and Reference Book.*

14. Quotations from U.S., Department of Defense, "They Speak for Themselves: Statements [on Housing Discrimination] by Military Personnel in the Metropolitan Washington Area," unpublished.

live is at least ten years old or possibly older, [has a] faulty electrical system, steam heat supplied by an old coal furnace, washers
and d[r]yers seldom not [sic] in operating condition due to being
constantly vandalized but I still have to pay $120.00 plus utilities
(electricity and cooking gas) monthly. I more or less had to accept
this neighborhood because I am not at liberty to undertake the
role as a CRUSADER for fair housing or other civil rights for which
I have raised my hand to *defend.*

4. August 1965—I attempted to find housing close to base in Maryland. The housing I checked had advertised vacancies. Phone
conversations with the resident managers confirmed vacancies.
But when I checked in person, I was greeted with the same problem so many Negroes have when they try to get off-base quarters
close to the base. "I'm sorry [,] sir, but we do not rent to colored."
So I found suitable housing in S. E. Washington. Rent was higher
and I had to drive further, but I had no racial problem. Fourteen
months later I was lucky to get on-base housing (October 1966).
I'm very pleased with my present quarters.

Of the white servicemen polled by the Defense Department, some
showed great sensitivity to the black soldier's plight. Said one:

If the military service is unwilling or unable to provide adequate and
sufficient housing on every base to which its personnel are assigned,
it should provide on-base housing based on different criteria then
[sic] are now in effect. Instead of rank or position as the primary
criteria, I would think priority should be given to minority groups
and families with large numbers of children. . . . The people who
are generally most capable of obtaining housing which is suitable
for them (i.e., white, higher ranking personnel) inappropriately get
priority.

Said another:

I am Causcasian [sic]. I first looked for an . . . apartment near Walter
Reed [in Washington], in Arlington [Virginia], and Prince George's
County [Maryland]. I quickly found out the majority (and all the nice
ones—the new ones) were segregated. When they denied they were
segregated and knew that I wanted integrated housing, they said
they had a long waiting list ahead of me. (This was true even for
one apartment house which had three vacant apartments just twelve
hours before.) I then sought an integrated apartment house in the
district [of Columbia] where they (theoretically) have a fair housing
law. If I did not initially make clear I wanted integrated housing, the
resident nanager of most of the apartments on Connecticut Avenue,
N.W. and Tunlan and Wisconsin Avenues, N.W. would say that
they were segr[eg]ated ("We keep those niggers out, thank God").

One place on upper Connecticut Avenue (informally) united action to get around the law. When I (politely) made known my wishes for integrated housing I was called a "troublemaker" and was refused further consideration. This search has caused me great inconvenience. The Department of Defense should take firm leadership in securing equal opportunity for military housing off-base.

Lest it be imagined that these complaints are confined to Southern or border states such as Maryland, the same Pentagon document from which the above quotations are taken has an abstract, "Case Number 28," submitted sometime between the spring of 1966 and the spring of 1967, which states:

> The Commander of a large military installation in a populous Midwest center reports that the large majority of off-base housing is segregated. Negro members and their families who reside in off-base housing live in areas that are predominantly all Negro. *Many of the Negro base personnel have to travel a round trip of 80 to 86 miles per day to come from their residence to their duty station. Discrimination in off-base housing in this Northern Midwestern community is more rigid than in any of the thirteen communities, including many in the South,* that were visited by Joint DOD-Military Department Teams. Not only was there residential segregation in this area, but there were many reports to the Commander of discrimination and segregation in public accommodations such as restaurants, taverns, night clubs, hotels and motels.[15]

The problem is in fact nationwide, as one would suspect and as the Defense Department confirmed when in the spring of 1967 it extended its Washington area survey of equal opportunities in off-base multiple-unit housing to all military installations in the continental United States to which 500 or more servicemen are assigned. Completed in the summer of 1967, the census revealed that servicemen were discriminated against in at least a third of the facilities. This was true even in states such as California, which have so-called fair housing laws.[16] (See Table 4 for an alphabetical listing of the states.)

What has the Department of Defense tried to do about this evident racial discrimination? While using three approaches simultaneously, the Pentagon has changed its emphasis from friendly persuasion (which usually doesn't work) to a formal listing system (which works

---

15. Ibid. Italics mine.

16. U.S., Department of Defense, Office of the Assistant Secretary for Public Affairs. News Release No. 842–67 (Washington, D.C., 7 September 1967), p. 1. A specific example of California discrimination was the El Centro Naval Air Facility. The survey taken there showed that 44 percent of the landlords in the area of the base discriminated against black sailors and their families. *Washington Post*, 20 September 1967, p. 2.

TABLE 4
Defense Department Survey
of Off-Base Housing

State	All Facilities[a]		Apartments		Housing Developments		Mobile Courts	
	Total	% Open	Total	% Open	Total	% Open	Total	% Open
Nationwide	25,180	67	21,014	67	946	75	2,859	66
Alabama	225	48	113	38	40	77	71	45
Arizona	287	91	235	94	2	100	50	78
Arkansas	83	72	54	74	00	0	29	69
California	14,429	68	13,428	69	212	76	592	63
Colorado	535	90	469	90	16	100	50	94
Connecticut	53	100	21	100	—	—	32	100
Delaware	36	61	15	80	3	67	18	44
Florida	654	52	477	51	26	85	149	50
Georgia	501	35	270	29	69	54	161	36
Idaho	35	93	20	90	4	100	6	100
Illinois	461	51	340	49	59	63	61	52
Indiana	203	76	158	75	1	100	44	77
Iowa	31	74	20	75	—	—	11	73
Kansas	280	68	76	64	29	38	75	88
Kentucky	125	77	48	71	14	64	31	90
Louisiana	270	34	201	23	27	48	42	79
Maine	215	89	200	89	2	100	12	92
Maryland	361	44	264	42	26	22	71	62
Massachusetts	104	93	71	94	7	100	26	88
Michigan	144	72	116	67	3	100	25	88
Minnesota	140	96	129	96	1	100	10	100
Mississippi	81	49	46	28	14	100	21	62
Missouri	182	77	85	71	50	94	40	68
Montana	93	59	64	48	12	92	17	76
Nebraska	60	70	46	65	—	—	14	86
Nevada	95	85	61	93	—	—	34	71
New Hampshire	30	100	14	100	—	—	15	100
New Jersey	114	97	124	96	—	—	20	100
New Mexico	260	83	200	82	15	100	45	82
New York	207	99	151	99	1	100	55	98
North Carolina	257	52	87	46	50	62	119	51
North Dakota	122	93	74	97	25	92	21	90
Ohio	105	77	69	86	2	100	34	59
Oklahoma	371	68	258	65	37	92	76	66
Oregon	78	100	55	100	2	100	21	100
Pennsylvania	139	89	107	95	5	100	27	63
Rhode Island	151	91	103	89	23	91	24	100
South Carolina	469	40	235	39	50	85	184	29
South Dakota	47	100	30	100	—	—	17	100

TABLE 4
(continued)

State	All Facilities[a]		Apartments		Housing Developments		Mobile Courts	
	Total	% Open	Total	% Open	Total	% Open	Total	% Open
Tennessee	68	64	37	59	4	100	27	65
Texas	1,004	72	730	68	72	82	201	82
Utah	197	80	166	77	2	100	29	100
Vermont	—	—	—	—	—	—	—	—
Virginia	915	38	779	35	18	55	110	58
Washington	850	70	710	67	21	90	119	84
West Virginia	—	—	—	—	—	—	—	—
Wisconsin	15	100	15	100	—	—	—	—
Wyoming	68	91	43	93	2	100	23	87

[a]Total number of facilities vary slightly in some cases from sum of facility types because not all facilities were coded as to type.

a little) to the threat or use of economic sanctions (which works best of all). Under the formal listing system instituted by former Secretary of Defense Robert S. McNamara, owners of rental properties near military bases must sign agreements stating that they will not discriminate against military tenants with regard to religion or race. Otherwise they are not allowed to list their properties with base housing referral offices. Under an order issued by Clark M. Clifford, McNamara's successor, no member of the armed forces is allowed to lease or rent in trailer courts or multi-unit apartment houses anywhere in the United States if the owner discriminates against servicemen. If a serviceman desires, he can ask military authorities for legal advice including help in beginning a lawsuit against a discriminatory landlord.[17] As for results, Secretary Clifford claimed in mid-1968 that 83 percent of rental housing near military bases was open to minority groups as compared to something over 60 percent the previous year.[18]

There are, of course, "still stubborn pockets of resistance in many sections of the nation" and sometimes "the patterns of rigid non-

17. See Appendix I, "Civil Rights Complaint and Request for Suit," of U.S., Army, *Equal Opportunity and Treatment of Military Personnel.* Regulation No. 600–6 (Fort Meade, Maryland: First Army Headquarters, 14 November 1966).

18. *New York Times,* 21 June 1968, p. 24. See ibid., 31 December 1967, p. 37; and U.S., Department of Defense, *Resource and Reference Book,* p. 70, for more detailed comparisons.

compliance and noncooperation defy all of the previous thinking or conceptions about race relations and the acceptance of minority groups."[19] In struggling with open housing, the Pentagon has discovered a sad truth. It has discovered that as far as their attitudes toward blacks are concerned, many white Northerners are really Southerners in disguise, who just happen to have been born or who live in the North. In many cases their attitude is far worse than the white Southerner's. In some Southern communities, reports the Defense Department,

> there appears to be more willingness on the part of local leaders and owners and operators of rental facilities to make adjustments and comply with Department of Defense policies, while in Northern and Midwestern regions we are often confronted with a solid wall of resistance. Break-throughs are few, encouragement is little and progress slow.[20]

One can speculate as to why it is sometimes easier to "dediscriminate" in the South than in the North. For one thing, white Southerners have closely interacted with large numbers of blacks for a long time. This is a relatively new experience for Northerners. For another, even reactionary white Southerners admit the existence of a race problem (which they want to solve in their own special way), while even many liberal white Northerners ignore the problem if they can. And the third and probably most effective reason is that, compared to other parts of the country, the economic impact of military installations on many Southern communities is substantial. The impact at Fort Benning on Columbus, Georgia or of Fort Bragg on Fayetteville, North Carolina is much greater than is Fort Hamilton's on Brooklyn or Fort Dix's on South Jersey. Placing civilian housing "off limits" is a much more seriously felt sanction in the former communities than it is in the latter.

Two areas where the military has been less successful in raising the percentage of blacks are the National Guard and the officer corps of the regular forces.

The plain fact is that the National Guard is a segregated institution. It has always been so. It is so now. In 1964 only 1.45 percent of the Army National Guard was black. In 1968 even this tiny percentage went down (as shown in Table 5) to 1.26. The only Northern state to register any significant increase between 1967 and 1968 was New Jersey, which as an experiment was given a 5 percent over-

---

19. U.S., Department of Defense, *Resource and Reference Book*, p. 63.
20. Ibid.

TABLE 5

Negro—White Ratios
in the Army National Guard

State	Total personnel	Total Negro personnel 1967	Total Negro personnel 1968	Percent total 1967	Percent total 1968	Percent of population
Alabama	15,303	14	12	0.1	0.1	30.0
Alaska	1,827	11	9	0.6	0.5	3.0
Arizona	2,839	18	19	0.6	0.7	3.3
Arkansas	8,035	8	64	0.1	0.8	21.8
California	20,806	362	368	1.6	1.8	5.6
Colorado	3,011	4	12	0.1	0.4	2.3
Connecticut	6,128	27	18	0.4	0.3	4.2
Delaware	2,797	69	55	2.2	2.0	13.6
Dist. of Col.	1,703	446	370	25.7	21.7	53.7
Florida	8,144	29	55	0.4	0.7	17.8
Georgia	8,838	13	14	0.2	0.2	28.5
Hawaii	960	3	3	0.1	0.3	0.8
Idaho	2,732	0	1	0.0	0.1	0.2
Illinois	11,045	625	516	5.5	4.7	10.3
Indiana	10,240	83	55	0.7	0.5	5.8
Iowa	6,990	7	9	0.1	0.1	0.9
Kansas	4,115	46	17	0.6	0.4	4.2
Kentucky	4,525	28	20	0.5	0.4	7.1
Louisiana	7,888	32	44	0.4	0.6	31.7
Maine	2,765	3	1	0.1	0.1	0.3
Maryland	6,472	273	241	4.2	3.7	16.7
Massachusetts	14,389	58	64	0.4	0.4	2.2
Michigan	10,050	144	136	1.5	1.4	9.2
Minnesota	9,741	13	10	0.1	0.1	0.7
Mississippi	10,365	1	1	0.0	0.1	42.0
Missouri	8,656	72	59	0.8	0.7	9.0
Montana	2,562	4	3	0.1	0.1	0.2
Nebraska	4,354	5	3	0.1	0.1	2.1
Nevada	1,120	8	6	0.7	0.5	4.7
New Hampshire	1,760	0	1	0.0	0.1	0.3
New Jersey	14,256	611	823	4.1	5.8	8.5
New Mexico	3,305	19	16	0.6	0.5	1.8
New York	24,143	493	426	2.0	1.8	8.4
North Carolina	10,666	62	64	0.6	0.6	24.5
North Dakota	2,645	0	0	0.0	0.0	0.1
Ohio	15,091	255	201	1.6	1.3	8.1
Oklahoma	8,489	103	91	1.1	1.1	6.6
Oregon	7,623	13	18	0.2	0.2	1.0
Pennsylvania	18,013	295	252	1.6	1.4	7.5
Puerto Rico	6,623	640	501	9.2	7.6	—
Rhode Island	3,159	15	18	0.5	0.6	2.1
South Carolina	10,019	16	16	0.1	0.2	34.8
South Dakota	3,725	2	3	0.0	0.1	0.2

TABLE 5
(continued)

State	Total personnel	Total Negro Personnel 1967	1968	Percent total 1967	1968	Percent of population
Tennessee	10,523	73	62	0.6	0.6	16.5
Texas	16,905	62	131	0.4	0.8	12.4
Utah	4,554	2	2	0.0	0.1	0.5
Vermont	2,625	2	2	0.1	0.1	0.1
Virginia	7,663	17	31	0.2	0.4	20.6
Washington	6,099	30	27	0.5	0.4	1.7
West Virginia	3,385	61	63	1.7	1.9	4.8
Wisconsin	9,602	6	10	0.1	0.1	1.4
Wyoming	1,600	1	1	0.1	0.1	0.7
Total	390,874	5,184	4,944	1.24	1.26	10.0

Source: New York Times, March 24, 1969, p. 90 © 1969 by the New York Times Company. Reprinted by permission.

strength allowance by the Pentagon and mounted a publicity campaign to attract blacks to its National Guard ranks.[21]

There are reasons, if not justifications, for this segregation. Despite its name and overwhelming financial support from the federal government, the National Guard is basically a highly politicized state agency under state and local control. Only when a unit is federalized by the President is there even a possibility of a wider influence on the attitudes and mores of its members, and this only for a very short time. Thus, all of the race and color biases of the local residents are usually reflected in each unit.

William A. McWhirter showed this in an article he wrote on his experiences as a Guardsman.[22] "As a Guardsman, I heard the Negro called a reindeer, a Mau Mau, a jig, a spook, a brownie, a warrior, a chocolate man, a boon, a spade and a nigger." One Guardsman characterized riot control training as: "We're gonna kill niggers, that's what it's all about." When a sergeant began a riot control class with "Any questions?" the unit joker asked "Who's gonna play the nigger?" An Alabama Guard officer began his class with:

21. The overall black percentage for 1964 is taken from Stillman, *Integration of the Negro in the U.S. Armed Forces*, p. 97. For more details on the New Jersey program, see *New York Times*, 8 January 1969, pp. 1, 12; and U.S., Army and Air Force, *Annual Report: Chief, National Guard Bureau, Fiscal Year 1968* (Washington, D.C., 1968), p. 24.

22. From "Favorite Haven for the Comic Soldier," by William McWhirter, *Life* Magazine, 27 October 1967, pp. 86–98. © 1967 Time, Inc.

Do any of you know what a Nigger–Jew—I hope we don't
  have any Jews in here—is?

Nooo, sir.

He's a man who's so frustrated when he walks into a store
  he doesn't know whether to jew the price down or loot
  it.

To the extent that these anecdotes reflect widespread prejudice
throughout the states, it is doubtful how much devices such as the
National Guard Bureau's Office of Equal Opportunity and Civil Rights
and the New Jersey program can actually help. Even when prejudice
is absent or belated efforts to remove it are sincere, Vietnam-induced
pressures for Guard membership to avoid the draft, "the long history
of Negro exclusion, the [antimilitary] views of the present Negro leadership, and the more attractive uniformed service in the regular military" work against attracting suitable black candidates for Guard
membership.[23]

This is a pity. For even the Kerner Commission, established by
President Johnson to study the nation's racial disorders after the
Newark and Detroit riots of 1967, argued that because "of the limitations of state police and the restrictions on the use of federal forces,
the National Guard in state status is the only organization with sufficient manpower and appropriate organization and equipment to assist local police departments in riot control operations."[24] And because the Detroit evidence showed that the higher percentage of
blacks in the active army units used contributed significantly to the
less violent and more effective efforts of these units as compared
to those of the National Guard, the Commission called for more black
soldiers and airmen in the Guard.

If the percentage of blacks in the National Guard is low, it is
not very much higher in the officer corps of the regular services.
As of September 1968, only 8,600 officers, or about 2 percent of the
total corps, were black (see Table 1). Twenty years earlier, the situation
was worse. There were only 1,306 black officers in the army, 310
in the air force, four in the navy, and but one in the marine corps.[25]
Today, with only one black general in the army (Brigadier General
Frederic E. Davison), one retired from the air force (Lieutenant General
Benjamin O. Davis, Jr., himself the son of the first black general in
American history), no black generals or full colonels in the Marine
Corps, no black admirals and only three black captains in the navy,

---

23. Stillman, *Integration of the Negro in the U.S. Armed Forces*, p. 106.
24. *Report of the National Advisory Commission on Civil Disorders* (New York:
Bantam Books, 1968), p. 497.
25. *New York Times*, 27 July 1968, p. 28.

and only approximately 50 black officers above the rank of lieutenant colonel in all the armed services combined—one can only describe the present situation as tokenism.[26]

And the reasons for this? Commissioned officers are usually required to have college degrees. Relatively few black people do. And those young blacks who have them, don't generally pick the military as a life's career. This itself results from a combination of factors. First, formal segregation and discrimination before President Truman's landmark Executive Order 9981, issued on 26 July 1948, militated against a tradition growing up within the black community to encourage young men to enter the officer corps. Second, current antimilitary feeling among all colors of high school and college youth do nothing to strengthen that tradition. Third, there are the increasingly better job offers from universities, private industry, and civilian government agencies. Fourth, there are the pressures from black middle- and upper-income parents, who are often just as negative about their sons' choice of a military career as is perhaps the majority of white parents who have "made it." And an emerging fifth reason is the rising campus sentiment against ROTC, from which the army receives by far the largest portion of its officers. (To the extent that black officers enter the services through ROTC, any acceleration of the twin trends to remove academic credit for ROTC training and to extricate the ROTC program altogether from college campuses can only hurt the goal of having more black officers in the military.)

Promotion and assignment to the better jobs and better locations are a special problem for the black officer. Like his white counterpart, he wants to have equal expectation of steady advancement with his advancing years of service. If he is among the most capable, he wants to be able to dream the same dream of "making general." Yet the competition here is ferocious. For example, in 1967 only 72 army colonels were promoted to brigadier general from the more than 4,200 who were eligible.[27]

Promotion to the highest ranks is determined by selection boards. Assuming the absence of race prejudice (which one cannot always do), what impresses the boards most is whether the candidate has continuously acquired and applied technological and managerial skills, is a graduate of at least one prestigious senior service school (the National War College, Industrial College of the Armed Forces, Army War College, Naval War College, or Air War College), and wears the "old school tie" of a service academy. Black officers suffer on all three counts. Because of a late start and previous prejudice and discrimination, they do not generally have as much to offer technically and managerially as do white officers. As for senior school attendance,

---

26. See Alex Poinsett, "The Negro Officer," *Ebony* 23 (August 1968), pp. 136–41.
27. Ibid., p. 137.

only one black officer was enrolled in 1967—in the Army War College. That year also saw only two blacks graduate from the Military Academy, two from the Naval Academy, and one from the Air Force Academy.[28] The situation is improving. In 1968 alone there were more black cadets at West Point, Annapolis, and Colorado Springs—116—than the total number of 86 blacks who graduated from all three places between 1877 and 1965. But whether the situation is improving fast enough is the real point.

There are pluses and minuses in the military's efforts to bring equality to America's blacks and other minorities both on the base and beyond its front gate. A tragic, backsliding minus were the racial fights among servicemen in the summer of 1969, particularly at Marine Corps bases.[29] They still occur occasionally. But the pluses do on balance outnumber the minuses. And here lies the irony: the least democratic, most criticized American governmental institution today leads the others in fashioning a social policy that may in time bring true racial equality to the entire land.

---

28. These statistics, as well as the remaining ones in this discussion, are from U.S., Department of Defense, *Resource and Reference Book*, pp. 36–38, 43; Stillman, *Integration of the Negro in the U.S. Armed Forces*, pp. 68–69; and *New York Times*, 27 July 1968, p. 28.

29. For details, see Carl Rowan's column in the *Philadelphia Bulletin*, 27 August 1969, p. 17; Jack Anderson's column in ibid., 24 September 1969, p. 100; "Black Power in Vietnam," *Time* (19 September 1969), pp. 22–23; and *New York Times*, 10 August 1969, p. 67; 12 August 1969, p. 23; 17 August 1969, p. 54; 4 September 1969, p. 39; 14 October 1969, p. 21.

4

Military Conscription
and Non-Military National Service*

Except for the Vietnam War and the military-industrial complex, probably no military subject engages more of the public's attention than does the Selective Service System. Each year it spreads itself over the lives of the almost 2 million men who annually reach 19 years of age. Of these, about 1.3 million possess the mental and physical standards set by the military. However, only an average of about 300,000 have been drafted during each year of the Vietnam War, out of the 600,000 to 1 million men that have been required for duty.[1]

America's draft policies can be viewed from several vantage points. But no matter from which vantage point one does so, three facts are very clear. The first is that except for certain classes of conscientious objectors, the concept of involuntary service to the nation has been applied only to military service. The second is that women have been excluded from that concept, no matter how it has been applied. And the third is that a young male, if he is wealthy enough, intelligent enough, and lucky enough to get into and remain in a college or university can delay his military obligation at least until he has earned his bachelor's degree. If he marries and has children,

---

*A shorter version of this chapter appears in the December, 1969 issue of *Military Review* and material from it is reprinted by permission.

1. *New York Times*, 13 April 1969, p. 4.

engages in occupations his draft board may consider essential (such as public school teaching or agriculture), or enters certain graduate programs (which are again a function of money and brains), he can often delay his obligation indefinitely or escape it entirely.

This is not so true if the young man is a rural, low-income white who has not gone to college.[2] In 1964, for example, only 40 percent of all 26-year-old college graduates saw any military service whatever. During 1965 to 1966 "college graduates made up only 2 percent of inductees into the army, while men with high school or less education made up 85 percent of the total."[3] Nor is it so true if the man in question is a noncollege black man who meets the physical and mental standards of the armed forces. Only about one-third of the blacks who are examined are found acceptable for conscription. But two-thirds of the ones found acceptable are actually taken. This is the reverse of the situation that generally obtains for the whites.[4]

Our conscription policy has in fact been so heavily weighted in favor of the urban whites, the relatively wealthy, and especially the school-minded that it has given rise to an attitude best described as the arrogance of the intellect. That attitude expresses itself in a type of comment often heard on college campuses even before the Vietnam War: "What an absolute waste for a man of *my* intelligence to go into the military! Why, I'm much more valuable to society doing other things!"

Of course, this may well be true, but it may also be false. The country might indeed be better off if it produced more plumbers than physicists. At least plumbers don't design atomic bombs and other sophisticated weapons systems. And who knows how many young men who would really rather be photographers than physicians, chefs than civil engineers, or mechanics than mechanical engineers, chose college and degree-necessary careers solely in order to avoid or evade the draft?

In any case, the poor, the nonwhite, those individuals of any color who are permanently endowed with low I.Q.s, and those, again of any color, who are neither high academic achievers nor highly motivated to become so also have the right to fear and dislike a national obligation that may force them to kill and be killed. Those preparing for low-status occupations are just as entitled to feel frustrated and unhappy about an interruption of their careers as are people preparing for high-status ones. And in a democracy where is justice, morality, and fairness when so serious and dangerous an obligation as military

---

2. James W. Davis, Jr., and Kenneth M. Dolbeare, *Little Groups of Neighbors: The Selective Service System* (Chicago: Markham Publishing Co., 1968), p. 129.

3. Ibid., p. 15.

4. L. Deckle McLean, "The Black Man and the Draft," *Ebony* 23 (August 1968), p. 62.

service is in practice based on one's color, environment, motivation, and pocketbook rather than on more egalitarian criteria?

If this country faced the continuing military threat that is Israel's, we could probably introduce the fairness that her draft possesses because we would then conscript practically all physically fit 18-year-olds regardless of their intellectual capacities, color, career aspirations, or socioeconomic status. Like the Israelis, we would allow almost no one to go on to post-high school studies without a military discharge. Not only is the Israeli system fair. It has the virtue of letting the young man (and woman) know exactly what he or she will be doing in the 18- to 21-year-old time frame and to make postservice plans with a minimum of family and career dislocation.[5]

Happily, this country cannot adopt the Israeli system for at least two reasons. First, we do not have the special and immediate security situation that Israel has. We therefore do not need the military manpower requirements that such a situation produces. Second, short of the kind of mobilization demanded by World War II, a kind of war we shall probably never be called upon to fight again, America produces more 18- and 19-year-old males each year than we can really use for purely *military* service.

Almost everyone who seriously thinks about the American military draft system believes it to be unfair in important respects. Steps suggested for making it fairer range from drafting everyone (including girls) to drafting no one.[6]

The 1969 changes in the draft law still keep local quotas. However, selection is now geared to a national lottery of 19-year-old men, who are vulnerable for only one year. Undergraduate college deferments continue, but the college man must serve after graduation if his number was low enough.

Some of the draft's changes are fairer, if not always welcome. The random objectivity of the lottery replaces some of the loopholes, inequalities, and far from uniform judgements by local draft boards. This makes it possible for young men and the women they will someday marry to better plan their futures beyond their mid-twenties. It also reduces some of the planning problems of colleges and employers. But the draft is still limited to military service at a time when our domestic needs require a much broader approach.

What is needed is the inclusion of military service within the larger framework of national services and public acceptance of a definition of national service that includes nonmilitary and noncombat tasks at

---

5. See Edward Bernard Glick, *Peaceful Conflict: The Nonmilitary Use of the Military.* (Harrisburg, Pennsylvania: Stackpole Books, 1967), pp. 127–138.

6. See Sylvie Reice, "Let's Draft Girls as Well as Boys!" *Philadelphia Bulletin*, 10 May 1967, p. 90; and James C. Miller III, ed., *Why the Draft?: The Case for a Volunteer Army* (Baltimore: Penguin Books, 1968).

home and abroad. If we coupled this with a selection system that was both more equally applied and nationally useful, we would do a great deal to lessen the draft's injustices and simultaneously meet contemporary social needs within our country.

I suggest a *series* of lotteries and cutoffs involving both military and nonmilitary involuntary service to the nation. Generally, it would work as follows in the following order (see Figure 1):

1. All boys who reach 18 and who are physically and mentally fit would have their names placed into a *nongeographically* oriented military service lottery. If in accordance with the draft quotas for that year, or a lesser period, their names were drawn, they would be inducted into one of the three services for two years. The choice of the branch of service would also be by lottery, subject to the physical, mental, and numerical requirements of each service during the given period of time. Except for the direst of national emergencies, to be closely and clearly defined by law, a young man, having served the nation once, would never have to do so again unless he freely chose to reenlist into the military or volunteer for nonmilitary service.

2. Young men missed by the military lottery and all physically and mentally fit 18-year-old women would then have their names automatically placed into a series of nonmilitary lotteries in some order determined by the nation's needs in nonmilitary areas and by the physical, intellectual, or other requirements of these programs. There would be one lottery for the Peace Corps, another for the Teacher Corps, and still others for VISTA or new programs not now conceived or planned. One such program could be a Police Corps. Another could be a national Health Corps which would call up for service in city hospitals, slums, Indian reservations, and rural areas generally all categories of medical personnel from physicians, nurses, and technicians to orderlies.

3. Any young person whom the lottery chose for a program requiring more education than he or she possessed at the time would be allowed to pursue that education. But he or she would have to agree contractually to perform national nonmilitary service immediately upon the completion of studies. There would be no exemptions, only deferments of limited duration. If the young person, wanting to "get it over with," preferred not to go to college now in return for guaranteed national service later, he or she could ask that his or her name be placed into another nonmilitary lottery not requiring higher education or training.

4. Young people who could not meet the requirements of any of these lottery chosen programs, as well as any older or younger people not subject to the national service law, would by definition be recipients rather than givers of national service.

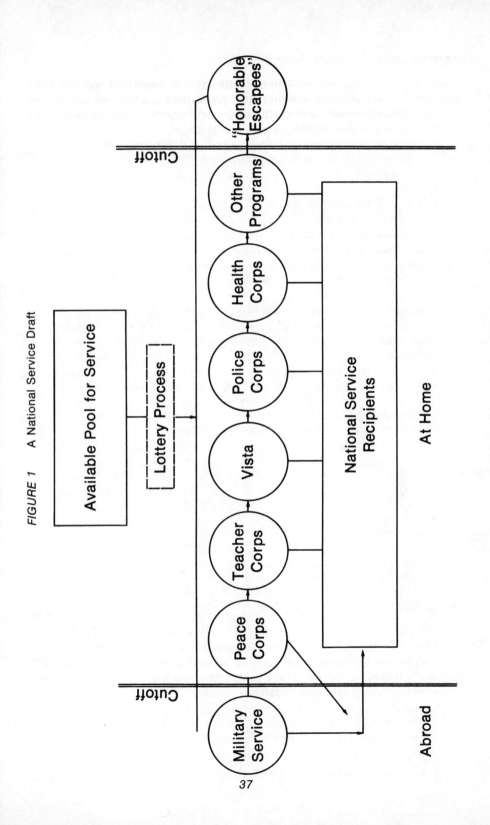

FIGURE 1 A National Service Draft

5. Since the median age of our population is getting lower, it is possible that the number of available youth will from time to time exceed the need for their services in all of the military and nonmilitary programs. In other words, some eligible young people may escape national service through the luck of the draw. But at least they will have escaped it more honorably and fairly than is often the case at present.

My plan undoubtedly has undiscovered flaws. These will hopefully be uncovered and eliminated as the plan is refined and administered. Some people will find in it unacceptable components or premises. The idea of police service in lieu of military service, for example, may be anathema to both peace and "law-and-order" groups, although Peter E. Yaeger argues the opposite:

I wonder whether the draft resisters and the "law-and-order" people have opened up a possibility that could help bring them, and the nation, together—namely, alternative service for the draft in the form of police work. . . .

The merits of such a proposal are obvious. It would give college graduates the chance to learn and do something about social problems which they are now content merely to demonstrate against, while directing the nation's greatest pool of talent against the problems of the cities rather than the jungle villages.

Police age and physical standards need not be relaxed, and if "corner sociologists" are what we need, standards in that regard would be much improved. If two years, the present draft tenure, is too short for police work, no doubt many graduates would consider an extra year of service a small price to pay for avoiding a war they detest. For potential lawyers, alternative police service would be a positive boon.

As for the "law-and-order" people, they should be more willing to see their sons walking the beat than patrolling the jungles; it's safer, more productive, and closer to home. . . .[7]

Others will object to the compulsory inclusion of women. Yet in 1967 Senator Edward M. Kennedy said: "Thousands, possibly millions, of young women would like a chance to help their country by performing recognized national service."[8] And in that same year 35 percent of the men and 33 percent of the women queried by the Gallup Poll answered the following proposition affirmatively:

There is an estimated shortage of 500,000 nurses, hospital aides and medical helpers in hospital[s] and nursing homes in the United

---

7. In a letter to the *New York Times*, 24 November 1968, p. E—13.
8. *Philadelphia Bulletin*, 10 May 1967, p. 90.

States. It has been suggested that young women be drafted to help fill these vacancies on the same general basis that young men are drafted for war service. Would you approve or disapprove of drafting young women for medical service?[9]

Still others will object to the plan despite its non-combat features, precisely because it is compulsory. Thus, one could not expect support from, say, the West Coast Quakers, who at their Yearly Meeting in California in the summer of 1968 resolved that

> conscription of any kind threatens the right and responsibility of every person to make his own decisions of conscience.
>
> We stand by those persons who refuse to perform unconscionable acts. We call for the abolition of the Selective Service System, and commit ourselves to work with renewed concern to abolish it.
>
> We are further concerned that conscription not be extended not even for constructive purposes, by such a system as national service. We will work to prevent the formation of any such system which would perpetuate conscription.[10]

But those who in good conscience don't want to abolish the draft but do want to make it fairer and more constructive may feel that my proposal warrants being tried at least on a test basis. For it does seem to have a number of advantages.

It would harness to nonmilitary and non-combat national needs the very obvious and considerable energy and idealism of the nation's youth. And it would do so without attaching stigmas and epithets to those young people serving in the nonfighting forces. It would tap the resources of the nation's young women, answering their cries for sexual equality with men by making their obligations more consonant with their rights. It would offer the government much more flexibility in dealing with conscientious objection to all wars in general and with selective conscientious objection to a specific war in particular. Finally, it would be fairer to blacks and other nonwhites than an all-volunteer army. For if white America continues to discriminate in civilian jobs against black America, but at the same time raises the salaries of military volunteers to a level that blacks do not receive in civilian life, then the percentage of nonwhites in the military will rise drastically. We may even see a nearly all-black army, and what will this do to the American concept of equal rights balanced against equal obligations?

---

9. Ibid., 22 February 1967, p. 9. However, the younger the respondents, the less they approved. Those 50 and over approved by 41 percent, those between 30 and 49 by 30 percent, and those between 21 and 29 by 27 percent.

10. *New York Times*, 25 August 1968, p. 4.

Like all policy proposals, this one is based on an assumption. The assumption here is that it is right and proper for the nation to expect from its youth a period of involuntary service to the nation. But it must give them both military and nonmilitary alternatives that are objectively arrived at and equally applied. This proposal does so in a way that will appeal to all citizens save those who believe that they owe the nation nothing in time or effort except what they choose to donate on a completely voluntary basis.[11]

---

11. Congressman Johnathan B. Bingham of New York has introduced a bill in Congress (H.R. 18025) which would give young men three options: "to volunteer for military service; or to volunteer for civilian service; or to take their chances on being drafted under a lottery system." See his letter to the *New York Times*, 29 June 1970, p. 34.

5

The Military
in Civilian Education
and Training

Every effective soldier, by his very task, must be a teacher.[1]

The American defense establishment runs the largest educational and training system in the world. In that system the average "military man probably devotes a larger proportion of his career to formal schooling than any other professional."[2] Because war is very technicized now, many of the courses he is given are for increasingly complex combat occupations. However, since successful military performance depends on nonfighting specialties ranging from meteorology to medicine and from literacy in one's own language to fluency in somebody else's, relatively fewer and fewer American servicemen over the years have been prepared for combat beyond basic training.

---

1. Morris Janowitz, *The Military in the Political Development of New Nations* (Chicago: University of Chicago Press, 1964), p. 81.
2. Colonel Robert N. Ginsburgh, "The Challenge to Military Professionalism," *Foreign Affairs* 42 (January 1964), p. 265. See also Albert D. Biderman, "Sequels to a Military Career: The Retired Military Professional," in Morris Janowitz, ed., *The New Military: Changing Patterns of Organization* (New York: Russell Sage Foundation, 1964), pp. 287–336; Harold F. Clark and Harold S. Sloan, *Classrooms in the Military* (New York: Bureau of Publications, Teachers College, Columbia University, 1964); John W. Masland and Laurence I. Radway, *Soldiers and Scholars* (Princeton: Princeton University Press, 1957); Harold Wool, "The *Changing* Pattern of Military Skills," *Employment Security Review* (July 1963), pp. 1–6; and Laure M. Sharp and Albert D. Biderman, "Out of Uniform," ibid. (February 1967), pp. 39–47.

During the Civil War 93.2 percent, and during the Spanish-American War 86.6 percent, of our soldiers were trained primarily for combat. But in World Wars I and II, in the Korean War, and in 1956 the percentages fell respectively to 34.1, 38.8 and 25.3. In 1968 only 12 percent had combat specialties, and an estimated 95 percent of those who left the air force did so with skills transferable to civilian society. Overall, one out of every six men now in the civilian labor force received occupational training in the nation's armed services.[3]

The influence of military institutions and events on American education is really not new. In the 1800s soldiers in the Northwest Territory were often teachers, and for a long time elementary schools on military posts were superior to civilian schools. That is why parents frequently asked for permission to send, and many did send, their children to these schools. In 1802 Congress established the Military Academy at West Point. For years it was the main science and engineering teaching center in the United States, supplying the very first engineering professors at our civilian universities.

The Civil War saw the passage of the Morrill Act, which established the land-grant colleges. One of the reasons for its passage was the expectation that these new colleges would teach "military tactics." Soon after the Civil War, the army instituted the practice of sending soldiers to civilian universities for more study, beginning first with medical and then with ordinance and engineering officers.

The First World War spurred demands for better academic, vocational, music, and physical education in the country. It also produced the War Risk Act of 1917, the Vocational Rehabilitation Act of 1918, and the schooling program which the army undertook in 1919 for troops awaiting return to the United States.

Among the civilian-oriented educational accompaniments of the Second World War were the Navy's V-12 program, the Army Specialized Training Program (ASTP), and the wide-ranging United States Armed Forces Institute, which still exists. USAFI has, among its other accomplishments, enabled millions of servicemen to earn high school equivalency certificates and diplomas. World War II also saw the birth of the GI Bill, the impact of whose educational assistance provisions were truly revolutionary. For the veterans it meant that millions who never would or could have gone to college (or other training centers) now had the money and the motivation to do so. For the colleges it meant vastly increased enrollments, year-round operation, experience with the conditional acceptance of the academically deficient, an older, more mature, and more motivated student body, and such arresting phenomena as on-campus villages filled with married stu-

---

3. Glick, *Peaceful Conflict*, p. 27, and William Leavitt, "Project 100,000: An Experiment in Salvaging People," *Air Force/Space Digest* (January 1968), p. 61.

dents, their wives, their children, and their problems. For society it meant a more educated, trained, and affluent electorate.

The 1950s and 1960s brought us the National Science Foundation, established partly because of the need for better national defense research, the National Defense Education Act, which federally supports civilian education in foreign languages, foreign areas studies, mathematics, and science, and the "impacted areas" program under which local school districts with large numbers of federal installations and military and civilian employees get extra financial aid. These years also brought with them the continuation of the draft, the Korean War and Vietnam War versions of the GI Bill, the ROTC controversy on college campuses, thousands of military officers on active duty who have taken advanced degrees at civilian universities, the even greater number of civilian college graduates who have filled the officer ranks through various routes, and the medical ministering of the Veterans Administration. (The VA runs the largest medical complex in the nation today with over 160 hospitals and clinics. It provides the internships and residencies for almost half of our graduating physicians. It annually trains some 40,000 dentists, nurses, social workers, audiologists, and other medical specialists. And in a recent typical year it treated almost 800,000 bed patients and 7 million outpatients.)[4]

Most important of all, the years since World War II produced the political habit of using the robe of national security[5] to clothe educational and training activities that might or might not be able to find nonmilitary justification and support. Two such activities are Project 100,000 and Project Transition.

Project 100,000 takes its name from the 100,000 servicemen with less than the military's usual educational, physical, and mental standards whom the program is designed to involve each year. It is a link in the chain that goes back at least to the Development Battalions of the First World War and to the Special Training units and Limited Service category of the Second World War. It is primarily a response to the fact that the military rejection rate for those men examined has been so high. In 1965, for example, 35.2 percent were rejected for physical reasons and 16.5 percent for mental or educational reasons, as indicated in Table 6.

Besides lowering the military rejection rate for its own sake, Project 100,000 has broader objectives. One is to learn how to train and use a category of people who would have to be mobilized into the armed forces in case of the most serious of future national emergencies. Another is to find ways to increase the motivation for career

---

4. Lyndon B. Johnson, "Our Pride and Our Strength: America's Servicemen and Veterans." Message to Congress, 30 January 1968, p. 8.

5. I am indebted for this term to Joseph S. Zaleski, a student in my seminar on the politics of national defense at Temple University.

TABLE 6

Annual Military Rejection Rate (1941 to 1967)

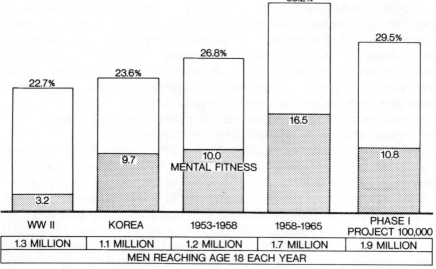

WW II	KOREA	1953-1958	1958-1965	PHASE I PROJECT 100,000
1.3 MILLION	1.1 MILLION	1.2 MILLION	1.7 MILLION	1.9 MILLION
MEN REACHING AGE 18 EACH YEAR				

success and to remove the conditions leading to career failure among soldiers with lesser backgrounds. A third objective is to spread the burden of military service more equitably, especially during protracted conflicts as that in Vietnam. The fourth is to discover just how much the military can do to retrieve men educationally and physically, not only for military service but for later civilian employment as well.

In 1964 there were already serious suggestions that the army accept as volunteers up to 60,000 draft rejects under President Johnson's War on Poverty. For a number of reasons—including some officers' objection to the establishment of a military "Moron Corps" and some congressional leaders' unwillingness to put the army into the "health, education and welfare business"[6]—the suggestions were a bit ahead of their time. They had to wait until 1966 and early 1967, when Secretary of Defense McNamara proposed, President Johnson approved, and Congress allowed the implementation of Project 100,000.

What are its operating principles? First, the overall percentage of Group IV men, those who scored between the 10th and 30th percentiles on the Armed Forces Qualification Test (AFQT), has been raised from about 17 to 24 percent. Second, while standards for ac-

---

6. *Washington Post*, 14 August 1964, p. A–1, and 15 October 1964, p. A–45.

ceptance into the services have been lowered, performance standards for graduation from the training courses and for retention in the military have not. To achieve this, instructors give extra time and effort to Project 100,000 men who need help. When necessary, they are "recycled" through all or part of a course until they reach and maintain satisfactory performance levels. Third, the men, euphemistically called "New Standards" men, are not, says the Pentagon, "singled out or stigmatized."[7] They *supposedly* do not know that they are somewhat different from other servicemen, nor is their training supposed to reflect their differences. Fourth, all of the services—not just the army—must take a share of the New Standards men.

The period from October 1966 to September 1967 marked the first phase of Project 100,000. Of the 49,000 men involved, the army took 38,135, the navy 3,696, the air force 3,949, and the marine corps 3,472. Table 7 is a statistical profile of this first group, when it entered service.

Altogether, more than 200,000 men have passed through Project 100,000. How have they done?

TABLE 7

Characteristics of New Standards Men

Average Age	21
Race:	
White	61.3%
Black	37.1%
Other	1.6%
Home Geographical Region:	
Northeast	17.2%
North Central	26.5%
South	41.8%
West	14.5%
Civilian Earning Level:	
Unemployed	29.3%
Less than $60 a week	26.6%
Prior Civil Convictions	8.5%
High School Graduates	43.4%
Failed or Repeated School Grades	56.1%
Average of Completed School Grades	10.5
Reading Ability:	
Average grade level	6.4
Below the 4th grade	14.1%
Below the 5th grade	27.1%
Below the 6th grade	41.8%

Source: Compiled from U.S., Department of Defense, Office of the Assistant Secretary of Defense for Manpower, *Summary Statistics on Project One Hundred Thousand* (Washington, D.C., October 1967).

---

7. According to I. M. Greenberg, Director of Project 100,000, in an interview in Washington, D.C., 15 May 1969.

Ninety-five percent have completed basic training, compared to 98 percent of the other men. Their attrition rate beyond basic training is 10 percent, compared to about 4 percent for other men taking the same courses. In other words, 9 out of 10 New Standards men graduate from formal skill courses. As we might expect, they do better in those courses that stress practical work and on-the-job training. They do worse in those demanding a great deal of reading, mathematics, and theory. Consequently, they perform most highly in courses that deal with combat and with the more simple technical subjects.

Despite this, however, the military services as a whole are still able to assign 60 percent of Project 100,000 people to occupational specialties that have "direct or related counterparts in the civilian economy."[8] In descending order, these are: food service and supply handlers, electrical and mechanical equipment repairmen, administrative specialists and clerks, craftsmen, communications and intelligence specialists, electronic equipment repairmen, and medical and dental technicians. From the viewpoint of overall social impact, it is terribly significant that well over a majority of Project 100,000 graduates are equipped to function economically after they leave the military services, probably at higher earning levels than when they entered.

If the psychologists are right about the importance of status and its relationship to self-esteem, then the promotions record of New Standards men may be significant. Here again, they are not very far behind the others. Enlisted men in all the American armed services enter at what is known as pay grade E-1. E-9 is the highest pay grade an enlisted man can reach. If we exclude those in Project 100,000 who are there because of medically remedial physical defects[9] and not because of lower mental or educational standards, we find that after 19 to 21 months 52 percent of the New Standards men are E-4s or higher. For other men the figure is 59 percent. This comparison is a military-wide average and not the average for each individual service, where technical requirements and promotion policies vary considerably. The range between the promotion rates of New Standards personnel and others is smallest in the air force (0.1 and 0.2

---

8. U.S., Department of Defense, Office of the Assistant Secretary of Defense for Manpower and Reserve Affairs, *Project One Hundred Thousand: Characteristics and Performance of "New Standards" Men* (Washington, D.C., March 1969), p. ix. I have relied heavily on this document and on a speech by I. M. Greenberg, Director, Project One Hundred Thousand, Office, Assistant Secretary of Defense (Manpower & Reserve Affairs) at an education conference sponsored by Congressmen Dingell and Ford in Washington on 9 May 1969.

9. This category deals with men with physical defects such as obesity, underweight, hernia, and hemorrhoids. Such men can be accepted into Project 100,000 if these defects can be corrected within six weeks of the start of treatment. See U.S., Department of Defense, *Medically Remedial Enlistment Program*. Directive No. 1304.11 (Washington, D.C., 5 December 1966 and 25 April 1967).

percent), greater in the army (69 and 79 percent), the greatest in the navy (1 and 47 percent).

The Defense Department argues that "in part, this [last] disparity is due to the fact that in the navy most New Standards men receive on-the-job training instead of attending a formal course, and thereby take longer to qualify for promotion. Another relevant factor is the requirement to pass a competitive navy-wide written test to qualify for advancement to grade E-4 and above."[10] This implies that just as disadvantaged pupils don't do well on written tests in civilian society, New Standards men don't do well on them in the navy. But since so many Project 100,000 men are nonwhite, prejudice—unspoken and unrecorded—may also be a reason for the lag in promotions. The navy has long been the most snobbish and conservative of all of our armed services.

Besides promotions, the military use other criteria to measure performance. Among them are the evaluations of one's superiors, disciplinary rates, and staying power, or attrition from active duty. Ninety percent of Project 100,000 men are rated good, excellent, or outstanding by those who supervise them. Their court-martial rate ranges only between 2.0 and 3.4 percent a year. And while their staying power is less than for other men, it is at a level which the Defense Department considers acceptable.

The term "attrition" excludes draftees and others who have satisfied their required periods of service and includes "separations and losses due to unsuitability, unfitness, misconduct, medical reasons, deaths, hardship discharges and other causes."[11] The combined experience of the four services shows that after 19 to 21 months the attrition rate for New Standards men is 11.6 percent, compared to 5.9 for other men. Table 8 shows that while relatively low for the army, it rises sharply for the air force, navy, and marine corps, respectively.

Most interesting is the fact, as indicated in Table 9, that the military staying power of Project 100,000 graduates is significantly higher for whites than it is for blacks and other nonwhites. This is a pattern that is consistent for each military service and for each group of New Standards men. Whether this is related to the belief of many nonwhite soldiers and sailors that they have better social and career opportunities in the military than in civil society is difficult to say, but it may very well be true.

One of the most impressive of Project 100,000's accomplishments is in reading level improvement, something which has obvious meaning for the postservice potentialities of individual servicemen. For the

---

10. U.S., Department of Defense, *Project One Hundred Thousand: Characteristics and Performance of "New Standards" Men*, p. x.

11. Ibid., p. xi.

TABLE 8

Military Attrition Rates after
19 to 21 Months of Service
(September 1968)

Service	New Standards	Control Group
Army	8.7%	5.1%
Navy	18.4%	6.7%
Air Force	13.9%	8.2%
Marine Corps	24.9%	10.7%

Source: U.S., Department of Defense, *Project One Hundred Thousand: Characteristics and Performance of "New Standards" Men,* p. xi.

TABLE 9

Attrition Rate of Project 100,000 Men
(September 1968)

Months	Whites	Nonwhites
22 to 24	12.7%	7.2%
19 to 21	13.6%	8.2%
16 to 18	12.2%	7.6%

Source: U.S., Department of Defense, *Project One Hundred Thousand: Characteristics and Performance of "New Standards" Men,* p. xii.

approximately 15 percent of the men who need it, Project 100,000 has a literacy and remedial reading program. It is a kind of military Head Start program. The army calls its version APT, or Army Preparatory Training. The air force has its RPP, or Reading Proficiency Program. The navy prefers the designation RLT, or Remedial Literacy Training. Depending upon the student and the service, the soldier or seaman receives between 90 and 180 or more hours of reading instruction over a three to six weeks period. The navy has established no fixed level of increased reading achievement. However, the army's goal is 5th grade or higher and the air force's is approximately the 6th grade. The results match the goals, for 80 percent of the men leave their courses able to read at between 1.7 and 2.0 grades higher than the 4th grade ability they had when they entered training. The men of Project 100,000 are thus far from being the "Moron Corps" that some predicted they would be.

Judging from all of the above data, Project 100,000 is an educational and vocational success.[12] Why? The answer lies in human psychology and the characteristics of the military environment. Remember

12. The control group data on which Project 100,000 comparisons are based include Mental Groups I and II, that is, above average men. The Defense Department indicates (in ibid., p. xiii) that "in later reports New Standards men will also be compared with average men (e.g., Mental Group III's) and upper Group IV men. It is anticipated that

that the average New Standards man as a civilian was unemployable, unemployed, or badly paid when he was employed. He had a poor education and even poorer motivation. Sometimes he had a police record. He had little pride and even less status. He was often a kind of free-floating socioeconomic outcast, perceived as a "nobody" by both himself and others.

When he entered the service and especially Project 100,000, what did he find? He found a highly structured, highly disciplined institution that is able, in the words of I. M. Greenberg, the Project's director, "to improve his work habits and instill pride, self-confidence and a desire to succeed. He is under our control for 24 hours a day. He cannot decide to quit when he wants to."[13] He found a uniform, an insignia, and a unit. He found heterogeneous training classes and the awareness that he was a "somebody" who could learn a job that was waiting for him when he finished his classes. And if he was one of those whom civil society had hurt by its painful and persistent prejudices against him, he know that, in the main, he could advance within the military without worrying about his race or previous social, economic, and educational level.

What Project 100,000 can be to the beginning of an enlisted man's military career, Project Transition often is to the end of it. Certainly the general public knows that hundreds of thousands of young men join or are conscripted into the uniformed defense establishment each year. But how many know that nearly a million leave it (alive) each year? And how many know that about half of them do not go back to their former jobs or take additional training and education under various programs of the Veterans Administration?

Project Transition is for this "other half." It is not for those returning military men who are physical therapists or laboratory technicians, for example, and who can find advertisements promising "excellent starting salaries" in magazines such as *The Journal of the Armed Forces*.[14] Instead, it is, in former President Johnson's phrase, "a path to productive careers" for those discharged and retired noncommissioned officers and men whose militarily acquired skills command little or no economic respect in the civilian marketplace.

The problem of making a returning veteran economically attractive in that marketplace is itself composed of two subproblems. First, low motivation, low educational achievement, low mental abilities, and the fact that our present draft laws and employment needs discriminate against the less educated all combine to increase the probability that

---

the performance differences will be even narrower when New Standards men are compared to those with average entrance scores on the Armed Forces Qualification Test."

13. From a speech by I. M. Greenberg at an educational conference in Washington on 9 May 1969.

14. *Journal of the Armed Forces* (18 November 1967), p. 9.

this very group of men will be among the first to see military service. Once in the service, and for the same reasons that herded them into it, they have a harder time qualifying for precisely those occupational specialties that are most easily and profitably transferable to civilian life. Project 100,000 tries to break this cycle at one end of a man's military career just as Project Transition tries to break it at the other end. Second, without any guidance to encourage geographic mobility, many of these men tend to go back to the urban and rural areas that have the fewest job opportunities. They either do not think, do not know, or do not care about this. When left completely to themselves, they often make geographical and employment decisions that only increase the difficulties of return and readjustment. Project Transition tries to deal with these two subproblems.

The target group that it is interested in consists of those men with from one to six months of service time remaining who won't be going to school under the GI Bill, who won't be returning to old jobs nor reenlisting, and who have the dimmest economic prospects outside of the military.[15] Priority is given in the following order to: (1) the combat-disabled, (2) combat arms specialists who learned no civilian-related skills during their tour of duty, (3) other soldiers, sailors, and airmen who likewise learned no such skills or who want to upgrade old ones, (4) military retirees in any of the above categories, (5) those who will try to make it on their militarily acquired skills but who want referral help in seeking civilian jobs, and (6) those who want to "retread" themselves by learning an entirely new skill or trade.

The Project's main educational aim is to provide high school equivalency to those who want and need it. Its vocational aim is to prepare returning serrvicemen for satisfying and good-paying jobs in labor-short areas. To achieve these aims, the Defense Department works with the Labor Department, the Department of Health, Education, and Welfare, the Post Office, and other federal agencies, as well as colleges, private industry, and state and local governments, especially police and health departments.

Project Transition began formally in January 1968, when the Defense Department arbitrarily set an annual goal of polling 500,000 men and actually counseling 300,000 of them about their postservice aspirations. Table 10 summarizes the cumulative results obtained by November 1968, the latest date for which figures are available.

Some of the figures in Table 10 are particularly interesting. The 4 percent dropout rate is a low one, much lower than the rate in civil society. It shows that, once in the program, a serviceman remains

---

15. The data on which the discussion of Project Transition is based come principally from U.S., Department of Defense, Office of the Assistant Secretary of Defense for Manpower and Reserve Affairs, *The Transition Program* (Washington, D.C., January 1969).

TABLE 10

Project Transition Summary
(January to November 1968)

Number of questionnaires administered	346,668
Number of men counseled	278,256
Percentage of questionnaired men who were counseled	81%
Number who desired training of those not reenlisting	152,742
Percentage of whites not reenlisting who desired training	70%
Percentage of nonwhites not reenlisting who desired training	79%
Percentage of whites who desired training who entered training	34%
Percentage of nonwhites who desired training who entered training	40%
Number who entered training	51,460
Vocational training percentage	75%
Educational training percentage	25%
Percentage of those who entered training who are white	81%
Percentage of those who entered training who are nonwhite	19%
Number in training on 30 November 1968	14,333
Those who completed training by 30 November 1968	35,137
Percentage who dropped training	4%

Source: U.S., Department of Defense, *The Transition Program*, p. ix.

highly motivated and committed to finish his course of training. The table also shows that the percentage of nonwhites who desired and entered training is higher than it is for whites and that the 19 percent nonwhite enrollment figure is higher than the nonwhite percentage in the total American population.

There are formal Project Transition programs on at least 55 army bases, 14 shore-based navy facilities, and 180 air force installations. The courses given fall into three categories: academic upgrading; job training and placement by and in the private sector of our economy; and training and placement by and in the public sector.

The academic portion of Project Transition is really an extension of the Defense Department's existing General Educational Development, or GED, Program. It allows men a last chance while still in the service to attain a specific level of formal education. If they successfully pass tests for the 8th grade level, high school graduation level, or first-year college level, they can get a Certificate of Equivalency, now recognized in all states.

One Transition-inspired idea is Project VAULT—Veterans Accelerated Urban Learning for Teaching—at Webster College in St. Louis. "Ignoring all normal screening standards, such as college board examinations and well-rounded background, Webster professors went to Fort Leonard Wood, Missouri, and sought out in workshops and bars black and white soldiers from poverty areas who were about to be discharged."[16] They did so in order to achieve two things: to give men a chance at a professional career, and to provide trained

16. *New York Times*, 5 September 1968, p. 23.

teachers from the slums for city schools in the belief that they would be more effective in the classroom than middle-class teachers.

The first group of 42 veterans was admitted in 1968. They ranged in age from 20 to 45. Seventy-one percent (or 30) were black, 24 percent (or 10) were white, 5 percent (or 2) were Mexican-Americans, 50 percent had a high school diploma, 24 percent had some college, 53 percent were single, and the rest had approximately one dependent each. While 40 percent dropped out after the first year, of the others, three are top math students and one is excellent in chemistry.

As for the second group of acceptees, 30 of the original 38 are still attending. Of these 30, the average age is 26, 93 percent are men, 93 percent are black, 7 percent are white, 67 percent have high school diplomas, 40 percent have some college, 60 percent are unmarried, and 12 have an average of 2.1 dependents. While about half the students in 1968 came from outside of Metropolitan St. Louis, all of the 1969 enrollees come from the area.

The VAULT curriculum stresses field study and other ways of acquiring information and insight besides reading. Among the courses offered are a Conflict Analysis Seminar, Black and White Social Problems, Humanities Seminar in American Civilization, Humanities Seminars in Asia, Europe, and Africa, and Urban Action Learning.[17] VAULT graduates are expected to earn diplomas and teaching licenses in three years, and Project Transition people hope that other colleges and universities will follow Webster's example. Although they claim that other institutions "are now planning similar types of programs," little is heard of them.[18]

Academic education is important,[19] but 75 percent of Transition servicemen want vocational training for jobs in industry and government. More than 50 big companies and 400 small ones cooperate here. Table 11 gives examples of skills the big firms teach, while Table 12 lists the kinds of on-the-job training which small businesses provide.

Project Transition officials say that industry's participation has been the "uniquely innovative aspect of the program." It continues, they argue, because it benefits all parties—the individual servicemen, private industry, and the military establishment. The serviceman "is

---

17. Donald W. White, Director of VAULT, in a letter dated 21 October 1969.

18. U.S., Department of Defense, *The Transition Program*, p. 19. One university that does have a similar program is Temple. It is called VIPS (Veterans in Public Service).

19. While not a formal part of Project Transition, the Defense Department also has "early release" programs to allow certain categories of officers and enlisted men to leave the armed services early in order to attend college or to take civilian teaching positions. See, for example, U.S., Army, *Reserve Components: Relief of Officers and Warrant Officers from Active Duty*. Army Regulation No. 135–173 (Washington, D.C., 31 March 1961), pp. 41–42, and "DOD Amends Program for College Early Release," *Commanders Digest* 4 (27 January 1968), p. 4.

TABLE 11

Examples of Training Provided by Major Companies

American Oil
  Service Station Manager
Equitable Life
  Insurance Salesman
  Personnel Manager
Financial Programs, Inc.
  Retail Sales
  Sales
  Management Finance
  Security Sales
Ford Motor
  Auto Mechanic
  Sales
  Assembly Line Foreman
General Electric
  Sales Management
General Motors
  Diesel Mechanic
  Frigidaire Appliance
  Appliance Repair
  Truck and Coach
  Collision Repair
    and Refinishing
  Delco Fleet Service
  Automobile Mechanic
General Telephone
  Telephone Repair
  Warehouse
Gulf Oil
  Station Management
Honeywell
  Computer Program
  Computer Maintenance
Howard Johnson
  Restaurant Management
Humble Oil
  Station Management
IBM
  Computer Systems Fundamentals
  Sales and Repair
  Office Machine Repair
  Technical Representative
  Electrician-Mechanic
John Hancock
  Salesmanship
  Insurance Sales
Lockheed Shipbuilding
  Pipefitter
Metropolitan Life
  Insurance Sales

Mobil Oil
  Station Manager
Montgomery Ward
  Auto Air Conditioner Mechanic
  Radio-TV Repair
  Security Clerk
  Sales Management
National Cash Register
  Electro-mechanical Concepts
Nationwide Finance
  Manager Trainee
  Financial Management
  Field Representative
New York Life
  Underwriter
  Insurance Sales
Northrop
  Aircraft
  Food Management
J. C. Penny
  Auto Mechanic
  Parts Control
  Maintenance
  Stock Clerk
Philco Ford
  Electrician Technician
RCA
  T.V. Repairs
  Data Processing
Ryan Aircraft
  Plastic Parts Fabrication
Raytheon
  Electrician Assembly
  Drafting
Robertshaw Control
  Salesman
  Clerk
Royal Typewriters
  Office Machine Repair
  Salesman
Seaboard Finance, Inc.
  Consumer Finance
  Management Trainee
Sears Roebuck
  Sales Management
  Shipping Receiving
  Credit Trainee
  Basic Electronics

TABLE 11

(continued)

Examples of Training Provided by Major Companies

Standard Oil of California
  Station Manager
  Service Station Operator
Volkswagen
  Auto Mechanic

Xerox
  Technical Representative
  Machine Maintenance
  Clerical
  Service Technician

Source: U.S., Department of Defense, *The Transition Program*, pp.41–42.

TABLE 12

Examples of On-The-Job Training
Provided by Small Businesses

Automotive
  Auto mechanics
  Auto services
  Air conditioning
  Body repair
  Auto parts
  Paint shop foreman
  Dispatcher
  Truck driver
Electronics
  Basic electronics
  Data processing
  Sales and repair
  Computer maintenance
  Electronics assembly
Clerical
  Accountant
  Typist
  Bank teller
  Bookkeeper
  Stock Clerk
Publishing
  Printer
  Draftsman
  Key punch operator
  Lithographer
  Multilith operator

Medical
  Dental lab technician
  Nurse
  Veterinary assistant
Trades
  Sheetmetalman
  Welder
  Pipefitter
  Machinist
  Carpenter
  Cabinet maker
  Fence installer
  Masonry
  Upholstery
  Carpet and tile laying
  Carpet maker
Miscellaneous
  Cosmetologist
  Burglar alarm repair
  Meat cutting
  Crane operator
  Boiler tender
  Horticulturist
  Barber

Source: U.S., Department of Defense, *The Transition Program*, p.43.

assured of standard work skills and an opportunity for a specific job. . . . Industry in turn not only helps satisfy its own manpower requirements, but . . . raises the skill and economic level of a significant number of servicemen who enter the national manpower pool." And the military gains by being able to furnish "specific civilian opportunities and pay scales which help men compare reentry to civilian life with possible continuance in the service."[20]

If Project Transition cannot operate without private industry, neither can it work without other, nonmilitary agencies of government. At the federal level, much of the actual course development and training is supported by the Bureau of Employment Security of the Department of Labor and the Office of Education in the Department of Health, Education, and Welfare operating under authority of the Manpower Development and Training Act. The Federal Aviation Agency helps airmen to obtain the FAA certification that is an absolute requirement for certain civilian jobs. The Civil Service Commission, the Veterans Administration, and the field offices of the Department of Commerce provide information and contacts for those seeking and offering other jobs. Additionally, a number of federal agencies absorb Transition graduates directly into their own ranks. Among them are the General Services Administration, the Department of Housing and Urban Development, the Agriculture Department, the Justice Department's Bureau of Prisons, and the Post Office, which is the largest federal employer of Transition people. Well over 11,000 have taken the course for carrier/clerk. About 600 of them enter the postal service each month.

At the state and local government levels, there are formal Transition programs in Arizona, California, Georgia, Illinois, Kansas, Kentucky, Missouri, Nevada, New Jersey, North and South Carolina, Rhode Island, Texas, Virginia, and Washington State. They are principally for paraprofessional posts in public works, health, education, recreation, and law enforcement. Police work is especially popular and has a high placement rate.

The authorization for this segment of Project Transition is Army Circular Number 635–3, dated 17 April 1968, which established the Civilian Police Recruiting Program. It lets police departments recruit on the base during both on- and off-duty hours. It allows publicity for off-base recruitment. And "within reason," servicemen can be made available for interviews with police hiring officials away from military installations. The army even supplies a suggested draft letter that soldiers interested in becoming policemen or state highway patrolmen can use in applying for these jobs (see Figures 2 and 3). The Civilian Police Recruiting Program also permits early release. To be eligible, a serviceman must be within three months of his scheduled discharge and have a firm written offer of employment or training from a recognized *public* police agency.

The number of police vacancies throughout the land has been estimated as high as 15,000.[21] So it is hardly surprising that more

20. U.S., Department of Defense, *The Transition Program*, pp. 21–22.
21. *New York Times*, 22 November 1967, p. 7.

FIGURE 2
Army–Suggested Draft Letter for Applying for Civilian Police Employment
(Obverse)

_____
(Rank, Name)

_____
(Organization)

_____
(Address)

_____
(Date)

_____
(Chief, Sheriff,
Commander)

_____
(City, County, State,
Sheriff, Department)

_____
(City, State Zip Code)

Dear Sir:
I am interested in employment with the _____ upon
                                              (Department)
my release from the military service. Although I am presently scheduled for separation on _____, I may be released up to 90 days
                        (Date of Separation)
earlier to begin my police career.

The information listed on the reverse is submitted for determination
as to whether I am qualified for a position on your force. If I meet
the initial requirements of your Department, I would appreciate it
if you would let me know as soon as possible. Also, please inform
me of any additional requirements such as physical and other examination.

I will be able to begin the necessary separation procedures once a
date has been fixed as to the start of my employment or training.

                                        Sincerely,

                                        _____
                                        (Signature)
                                        (Typed or Printed Name)

Source: U.S., Army, Headquarters, _Personnel Separations: Civilian Police Recruiting Program._ Circular No. 635–3 (Washington, D.C., 17 April 1968), p. 5.

FIGURE 3

Army-Suggested Draft Letter for Applying for Civilian Police Employment
(Reverse)

1. _____
(Name)

2. _____
(Age)

3. _____
(Home or residence)

4. _____
(Height)

5. _____
(Weight)

6. _____
(Vision—to include corrected)

7. _____
(Statement of general physical condition)

8. _____
(Civilian education)

9. _____
(Specialized civilian training)

10. _____
(Military education)

11. _____
(Military occupation)

12. _____
(Previous police background)

Source: U.S., Army, Headquarters, *Personnel Separations: Civilian Police Recruiting Program.* Circular No. 635–3 (Washington, D.C., 17 April 1968), p. 6.

than 40 major metropolitan police departments, including those of New York, Philadelphia, Los Angeles, and the District of Columbia, recruit regularly on military posts. The pilot project which developed into this nationwide program was led by Inspector Boyd T. Willard, personnel director for Washington, D.C.'s Metropolitan Police Department. Within five months of its start, he eliminated his department's 380-man deficit. He therefore feels that the Pentagon's program has "been a lifesaver to us."[22]

It may also help other police departments, especially those trying to add more blacks. As Table 13 suggests, there are few blacks on the police forces of major American cities. Nevertheless, these are the very places where racial tension is highest and the need to do something about it is the most urgent. There may not really be a direct causal relationship between high black percentages in urban police departments and low levels of racial unrest. (Baltimore and Chicago have relatively high percentages of black policemen and each of these cities has had racial unrest.) But if there is such a relationship, then the army's Civilian Police Recruiting Program and the police training portions of Project Transition should help.

TABLE 13

Negro-White Ratios on Eleven Metropolitan Police Forces

City	Negroes	Total Force
Baltimore	1,260	3,502
Birmingham	1	524
Boston	44	2,779
Buffalo	24	1,720
Chicago	2,940	11,761
Dallas	140	1,405
Detroit	170	4,876
Houston	45	1,509
Los Angeles	320	6,392
New York City	1,355	27,112
Philadelphia	1,260	6,300

Source: New York Times, 5 October 1967, p. 22.

One civil rights group that thinks so is the Lawyers' Committee for Civil Rights Under Law. Composed of such prominent attorneys as Burke Marshall, Arthur H. Dean, Whitney North Seymour, Louis F. Oberdorfer, and Cyrus R. Vance, it cooperates with the Department of Defense and local police officials to encourage and train black servicemen for civilian law enforcement work. On the other hand, it

22. Quoted in Lieutenant Robert W. Engelhardt, "Policing Up Recruits," Army Digest 24 (January 1969), p. 41.

is not very hard to understand why at least certain black militants are very critical of these efforts. At best, they see them as attempts to co-opt and lure the "brothers" into the ranks of the white "pigs." At worst, they are hypocritical efforts "to pit blacks against blacks . . . should violence flare."[23]

While Project Transition has shown that it can perform and that it has great promise, it has problems, too. It possesses almost no budget of its own, relying mostly on the resources of others in and out of government. It doesn't have enough qualified guidance counselors. The courses it offers aren't always responsive to the men's real desires, nor are they always available at the bases to which the men are assigned. And the several early release programs in the military, because of the shorter tour of duty which they by definition allow, cut into the pool of soldiers attracted to Project Transition.

Externally, there is society's slavish worship of "credentials," which often gets worse as one moves from dark blue to light blue to white-collar employment. Obviously, degrees, certificates, licenses, diplomas, and apprenticeships are important, and I am not suggesting their total elimination. But what I am saying is this: for programs such as Transition to succeed, society will have exhibit much more understanding, flexibility, and compassion than it has in the past. We all know that the veteran must adjust to the society to which he is returning. He has always had to do that. But society must also adjust to the veteran, and in ways more meaningful than the cash bonuses to veterans that so many state legislatures and citizens find so politically and psychologically gratifying. Especially is this true if the veteran was one of society's victims before he entered military service.

Will society, in its several segments, make this adjustment? Will, for instance, the labor unions yield when returning navy Seabees (sailors from *Construction Battalions*), Project Transition graduates, and other returning veterans begin knocking on their doors in ever-greater numbers? Or will the unions continue to insist on their outmoded apprenticeship programs and their discredited discriminatory practices?

Will state teacher certification agencies and local school boards tap the large reservoir of retiring military officers who say they would like to teach if given the chance?[24] Will they raise age requirements? Will they waive the methods courses and the supervised teaching courses that they now demand of even experienced military instructors with a master's degree in "civilian" subject matter?

---

23. *New York Times*, 1 May 1968, p. 14.

24. See Albert D. Biderman, "Sequels to a Military Career: The Retired Military Professional," in Morris Janowitz, ed., *The New Military: Changing Patterns of Organization* (New York: Russell Sage Foundation, 1964), p. 315; and Laure M. Sharp and Albert D. Biderman, "Out of Uniform," *Monthly Labor Review* (February 1967), p. 47.

Will those who rule over the Kingdom of Health Care make it easier for someone similar to navy hospital corpsman Martin Johnson to enter one of the branches of subprofessional medicine? Or will we be reading more stories such as the one in the *New York Times* which tells of his difficulty in getting a state license to be a *practical* nurse, not a registered nurse? It seems that most civilian nursing schools "give little credit for military training or experience even though his experience includes minor surgery and treatment of wounds under battlefield conditions" in Vietnam, where he served as a combat medic with the Marines for over a year.[25] Will the battle here be won by those siding with New York State Senator Norman F. Lent who argues: "If we are to overcome our manpower crisis, conventional notions of existing categories of health personnel must yield"?[26] Or will the victory go instead to those such as Dr. Henry I. Fineberg, executive vice-president of the New York State Medical Society, who feels that, no matter what, all military personnel must take additional schooling before they can be accepted into the subprofessional ranks of civilian medicine?

A final point: Congress and the public are largely unaware of military-sponsored training programs such as Projects 100,000 and Transition. This is due partly to the relatively negligible costs of such efforts. It is due partly to the greater publicity given to issues such as the Reserve Officers Training Corps and Pentagon-funded research on college campuses. And it is due partly to the nation's much greater interest and involvement in the critical question of the Vietnam War itself.

When Congress and the people find out and have time to reflect on military educational projects, what will their reactions be? Will they accept them willingly and approvingly? Will they increase their funding? Will they acquiesce, even unwillingly? Will they regard them as another tentacle that a militaristic octopus will use to encircle and strangle American society? Will they feel that these are good secondary missions for an institution whose primary mission is something else? Or will they adopt the rejecting tone and stance of Berkeley's Professor Marc Pilisuk, who sees in them something that smacks of Nazi Germany? Replying to an article by Professor Roger W. Little of the University of Illinois in Chicago, who approves of the military's role in basic education and youth socialization, he wrote: "Goebbels is said to have been a most reasonable sounding man. I could picture his defense of the Hitler Youth Corps and can find nothing in Roger

---

25. *New York Times*, 28 September 1968, p. 25.
26. Ibid.

Little's arguments for military education that would be unsuited to such a defense."[27]

Or will Congress and the people really not care at all?

27. "A Reply to Roger Little: Basic Education and Youth Socialization Anywhere Else," *American Journal of Orthopsychiatry* 38 (July 1968), p. 880. This is a response to Little's "Basic Education and Youth Socialization in the Armed Forces," ibid., pp. 869–876.

Pilisuk, who chose to juxtapose basic education under military auspices with the Hitler *Jugend*, may not know that the Jews of Israel see no such comparison. Their army has an excellent system of basic education. Israeli draftees who need it get 100 hours of Hebrew in their first month of military service. In their 33rd month of service, those who lack an elementary school certificate are sent to a special school in Haifa to get one. Using small classes, two gifted teachers to a class, teaching machines, movies, teaching days that last from ten to twelve hours six days a week, the army gets most of the men to the desired level. Ninety percent of the students come from disadvantaged families from such underdeveloped countries as Morocco, Iraq, Tunisia, Yemen, Turkey, Iran, Libya, Egypt, and Algeria. (Interview in Haifa with the commandant of the school, Lieutenant Colonel Yitzchak Ziv, 14 August 1968).

6

The Professor and the Pentagon

The dictionary defines research as "diligent and systematic inquiry or investigation into a subject in order to discover or revise facts, theories, applications, etc." It does not say that university people have to be the only ones to make all the discoveries and revisions. Yet there are still professors who hold to the quaint notion that only they do real research, and that if they don't do it, it doesn't get done.

They forget that a great deal of shoddy scholarship is produced on American campuses and that much respectable research comes from well-trained nonacademics working outside the universities. They forget that many Ph.D.s do not have and do not want university appointments. They forget that some of these people can work in great federal laboratories such as the National Bureau of Standards, famous nonprofit "think tanks" such as the RAND Corporation, or prestigious private industrial facilities such as the Bell Telephone Laboratories. For instance, Dr. Julius Axelrod, the American who shared the 1970 Nobel Prize for Medicine, is with the National Institutes of Health and not with one of our universities. And they forget as well that even in so terrifying a research area as biological warfare, the army is able to attract and retain over 150 people with doctorates at Fort Detrick, Maryland, and that the National Academy of Sciences "has no trouble" getting young scientists to compete for the dozen or so annual postdoctoral fellowships available at Fort Detrick in fields such as entomology and aerobiology.[1]

Whether American researchers work on or off the campus, or engage in war research, peace research, basic research, or applied research and development, they almost always have to rely on the more than twenty federal departments and agencies that regularly fund scientific and technological activity in this country. And the fact is that the Department of Defense plays a commanding part in this funding. As Table 14 shows, in fiscal year 1969 DOD accounted for 50 percent of the total obligated research and development funds, 60 percent of the development funds, 37 percent of the applied research funds, and 14 percent of the basic research funds. For basic research, it had a greater congressional appropriation than even the National Science Foundation.

Testifying before the House of Representatives Subcommittee on Science, Research, and Development, Dr. Frederick Seitz, then President of the National Academy of Sciences, gave some justification for heavy government support of research and for the researchers' need for it:

> [The] individual research worker in a typical university, industrial, or government laboratory usually needs about 2,000 or 3,000 square feet of laboratory space which could be amortized . . . over 20 years . . . at a cost of about $10,000 per year.
>
> When supported properly he requires about $50,000 per year for his research.
>
> I want to emphasize that today we are past the era of string and sealing wax in carrying through research. . . .
>
> If I have one major item of advice to offer here, it is to beg you to understand and support the typical, good, research worker whose financial requirements are relatively modest.[2]

As for colleges and universities specifically, 75 percent of all their sponsored research moneys comes from the national government.[3] And, as indicated in Table 15, the only single agency that gives them more money for research than does the Defense Department is the Department of Health, Education, and Welfare.

---

1. Seymour M. Hersh, "Dare We Develop Biological Weapons?," *New York Times Magazine* (28 September 1969), p. 29.

2. U.S., Congress, House of Representatives, *Government and Science: Hearings before the Subcommittee on Science, Research, and Development of the Committee on Science and Astronautics*, No. 8. 88th Cong., 1st Sess. (Washington, D.C.: U.S. Government Printing Office, 1964), pp. 12–13.

3. U.S., Congress, *Centralization of Federal Science Activities: Report to the Subcommittee on Science, Research, and Development of the Committee on Science and Astronautics*, p. 27.

TABLE 14

Estimated Federal Obligations for Research
and Development for Fiscal Year 1969
(in Millions of Dollars)[a]

Agency	Total	Basic research	Applied research	Development
All agency total	15,844	2,146	3,297	10,401
Departments:				
Agriculture	261	102	145	14
Commerce	90	28	35	27
Defense	7,944	290	1,343	6,311
Health, Education, and Welfare	1,327	413	795	112
Housing and Urban Development	18	—	6	12
Interior	208	51	111	46
Labor	12	2	7	3
Post Office	26	—	3	22
State	14	—	10	4
Transportation	291	17	64	210
Independent agencies:				
Atomic Energy Commission	1,436	324	96	1,016
Fed. Communications Commission	0.9	—	0.9	—
Library of Congress	2	—	2	—
National Aeronautics & Space Adm.	3,816	645	600	2,571
National Science Foundation	265	241	6	18
Office of Economic Opportunity	47	10	14	23
Office of Emergency Preparedness	0.7	—	0.7	—
Office of Science and Technology	2	0.4	0.6	0.9
Smithsonian Institution	15	15	—	—
Tennessee Valley Authority	8	—	6	2
Arms Control & Disarmament Agency	6	0.6	4	2
Veterans' Administration	49	6	42	0.7

[a]Rounded figures for all agencies except AID obtained from the National Science Foundation from preliminary data assembled for Vol. 18 of Federal Funds for Research and Development and other Scientific Activities, fiscal year 1968, 1969, and 1970. AID estimate from Vol. 17. of Federal Funds is included.
SOURCE: U.S., Congress, House of Representatives, *Centralization of Federal Science Activities: Report to the Subcommittee on Science, Research, and Development of the Committee on Science and Astronautics*, Serial B, 91st Cong., 1st Sess. (Washington, D.C.: Government Printing Office, 1969), p. 22.

Harvard's President Nathan M. Pusey, appearing before the same House hearings as did Dr. Seitz, told the congressmen exactly how heavily his own university leaned on the federal government. Though it accepts no classified research, Harvard, he said,

has noted a steady upward growth in the amount and proportion of federal funds in relation to its total expenses since World War II. As recently as 1952 to 1953, expenditures at Harvard on government grants and contracts amounted to $4.7 million out of total expenses of $36 million. In 1962 to 1963, 10 years later, the figure was $31.2 million of the university's total expenses of nearly $100 million. . . .

TABLE 15

Federal Support of Research in Colleges and Universities
(in millions of dollars)

Department or Agency	Obligations			Expenditures		
	1968 Actual	1969 Estimate	1970 Estimate	1968 Actual	1969 Estimate	1970 Estimate
Health, Education, and Welfare	700	713	705	653	592	666
Defense	219	247	274	235	252	275
National Science Foundation	221	210	255	207	224	243
National Aeronautics and Space Administration	130	119	101	151	130	109
Atomic Energy Commission	93	94	96	93	94	96
Agriculture	62	62	64	61	62	64
All other	60	63	76	56	60	66
Total	1,485	1,508	1,571	1,456	1,414	1,519

Source: U.S., Congress, Centralization of Federal Science Activities: Report to the Sub-committee on Sciences, Research, and Development of the Committee on Science and Astronautics, p. 27.

Though some areas of scientific activity at Harvard have a higher proportion of private money than do others, *none could carry on investigations on anything like the present level without federal aid.*[4]

That was in 1963. In 1968, the Year of the Riots, even a Columbia University committee which recommended more supervision of staff members who accepted private and government funds for their projects could not ignore this academic fact of life: "Columbia, alas, does not live by endowment alone, or even from investment income plus tuition fees. Many of the university's involvements result from its dependence on outside funds even for basic functions; some instruction and most research today are financed by outside contracts or grants."[5]

Universities in America have in a way the same need for government funds—often coming from military budgets—that men have for women. Both cannot live easily with them. Yet both can't really live without them. And like men, universities constantly complain about their problem, as indeed they should.

It engages several categories of people and issues. This is so even when there is no traumatizing national event as a Vietnam War to bruise and tear at the nation. Even in normal times we find debate

4. U.S., Congress, Government and Science, pp. 307–308. Italics mine.
5. Quoted in New York Times, 8 June 1968, p. 24.

between (and about) those in the university community who do research (and thus need money for it) and those who don't (and don't
need money for it). Often the argument here is framed as one between
the "teachers" and the "researchers," both of whom forget that the
ideal professor is the "teacher-scholar."

Among those professors who regularly do research the argument
is between those in "hard" fields (engineering and natural or physical
science) and those in "soft" ones (the humanities and the social
sciences), some of which are "harder" than others. Or it is (1) between
those who want and get federal funds and those who don't, (2) between those who are willing to take federal funds from the military
and those who will take them only from the "good" federal agencies,
or (3) between those who will take military money for basic research
that has no apparent or immediate military application, or for research
in a value-neutral, "motherhood" area as is medicine, and those who
seek and use Defense Department resources for value-laden social
science and national defense policy research and consultation.

What are some of the views in the Great Research Debate? J.
William Fulbright, chairman of the Senate's Foreign Relations Committee is one of the country's most articulate critics of the "growing
militarization of the economy and the universities."[6] In a statement
issued on 13 December 1967—one that does not always clearly distin-
guish between *government* funding and *military* funding and between
research for military purposes and for nonmilitary purposes—he said:

> The universities might have formed an effective counterweight to the
> military-industrial complex by strengthening their emphasis on the
> traditional values of democracy, but many of our leading universities
> have instead joined the monolith, adding greatly to its power and
> influence. Disappointing though it is, the adherence of the professors
> is not greatly surprising. No less than businessmen, workers and
> politicians, professors like money and influence. Having traditionally
> been deprived of both, they have welcomed the contracts and con-
> sultantships offered by the military establishment. The great majority·
> of American professors are still teaching students and engaging in
> scholarly research, but some of the most famous of our academicians
> have set such activities aside in order to serve their government,
> especially those parts of the government which are primarily con-
> cerned with war.
>
> The bonds between the government and the universities are no more
> the result of a conspiracy than those between government and busi-
> ness. They are an arrangement of convenience, providing the gov-
> ernment with politically usable knowledge and the universities with

---

6. This, as well as the other quotations from his statement, entitled "The War and
Its Effects–II," are taken from a copy supplied by Senator Fulbright's office.

badly needed funds. Most of these funds go to large institutions which need them less than some smaller and less well-known ones, but they do on the whole make a contribution to higher learning, a contribution, however, which is purchased at a high price.

That price is the surrender of independence, the neglect of teaching, and the distortion of scholarship. A university which has become accustomed to the inflow of government contract funds is likely to emphasize activities which will attract those funds.

In this same statement Senator Fulbright deplored "the taking into the government camp of scholars, especially those in the social sciences, who ought to be acting as responsible and independent critics of their government's policies." He claimed that what was going on was a "corrupting process" whereby "lucrative contracts are awarded not to those who question their government's policies but to those who provide the government with the tools and techniques it desires."

Senator Fulbright is not now an academician. However, his opinions would merit consideration regardless of whether he was on or off the campus. In any event, there are university scholars, as eminent, eloquent, and sincere as he, who both agree and disagree with his views in important respects. Thus, Professor Jerome B. Wiesner, now provost of MIT, but at one time director of the Office of Science and Technology and science advisor to President Kennedy, has declared:

I have said, and I hope you don't misunderstand me when I say this, that we in a sense were lucky in this country that we had the cold war in the period of the fifties. It gave us an automatic motivation to carry out a very intensive and extensive research and development activity.

These activities were carried out in the name of national defense by the Department of Defense and the Atomic Energy Commission, and we are very fortunate, I believe, that the people who had responsibilities for those programs recognized the deep dependence of applied research and technology on fundamental research. *They stimulated,* in parallel with the applied laboratories, *a growing basic research activity primarily in our universities.* I think we owe a great deal to them for their foresight in this. . . .

We also have the good fortune that much was done in applied areas that has great meaning, significance, and relevance to our civilian economy. I think we all appreciate the fact that we wouldn't have modern air transportation, either aircraft, or navigational facilities, had there not been the urgency of military applications. I doubt whether we would have modern computers of the quality we have, or many modern communication techniques, including television, if much of the basic research done in electronics hadn't been carried out and much of the applied research didn't have direct application.[7]

Professor Wiesner did add a very important caveat, however. While he believed in the 1950s and early 1960s that military support of scientific and technological research contributed to universities and to the country in many ways beyond the "primary reasons for the investment," it did not necessarily follow that "continued investments in military technology at any level will [always] be good for the country. I think one has to reexamine this whole problem of both direct investments on explicit purposes, and associated effects in other areas, because levels of spending are so much higher today [in 1963] that we may be at a place where we are substituting one set of goals for another."[8] This helps explain his later opposition to the deployment of an American antiballistic missile system.[9]

The former science advisor to President Nixon, Dr. Lee A. Du-Bridge, has stressed some of the same points in a different manner. Recalling history, which some students and their professors either ignore or are ignorant of, he said in a recent interview that at the end of the Second World War

There was no mechanism in the government at that time for the support of basic university research. The navy stepped in and, through its Office of Naval Research, said, "We will be the supporter of basic university research. . . ."

In the last two years, because of budgetary restrictions, the range of scientific activities being supported by the Office of Naval Research has been reduced. Some of its projects have been passed over to the National Science Foundation [which Congress did not establish until 1950]. But the point I am trying to make is that there is a misunderstanding on some campuses about the relationship of such agencies as the Office of Naval Research and the Office of Air Research, with the university community.

Those offices are supporting basic research, nonclassified, and disconnected from the immediate, foreseeable weapon and military applications. They are supporting it because they think contact with the scientific community is valuable, that the strengthening of the university and our scientific enterprise is valuable.[10]

7. U.S., Congress, *Government and Science*, pp. 61–62. Italics mine.
8. Ibid., pp. 64–65.
9. See Abram Chayes and Jerome B. Wiesner, eds., *ABM: An Evaluation of the Decision to Deploy an Antiballistic Missile System* (New York: Harper & Row, 1969).
10. *New York Times*, 17 December 1968, p. 30. Regarding DuBridge's point about post-World War II history, see Carroll W. Pursell, Jr., "Science and Government Agencies," in David Van Tassel and Michael Hall, eds., *Science and Society in the United States* (Homewood, Illinois: Dorsey Press, 1966), pp. 223–49.

A scholar who feels strongly that no good has come to basic research from the military is Professor Irwin D. J. Bross of the Roswell Park Memorial Institute and the State University of New York at Buffalo. He believes that

> In retrospect it is becoming increasingly clear that the money which is spent by the Department of Defense for "basic science" has been worse than wasted. . . . [This] output from DOD-supported "basic science" has contributed little or nothing to progress in the sciences and to the strengthening of the universities. . . .
>
> Moreover, few of the promised benefits to teachers or to students have materialized. When the bookkeeping is closely scrutinized it turns out that DOD research activities have in fact been parasitic—both academically and financially. . . .
>
> The influx of military funds has resulted in a steady erosion and debasement of the quality of "basic research." Thus, in some areas of science—computational linguistics, for instance—the influx of military funds has led to the growth of a blatant pseudo-science which is crowding out the genuine scientific work in the area.
>
> On the balance, I would say that military funds have done far more to cheapen and corrupt scientific research—to shift the emphasis from scientific competence to public relations skills—than they have done to advance the sciences. The dangers of military control over civilian science can be avoided in a straightforward way: all funds for "basic science" should be eliminated from Department of Defense budgets.[11]

One university scientist, Professor J. C. Phillips of the University of Chicago's Physics Department, has gone so far as to charge that "Scientists engaged in nonmilitary research at universities are solicited to consult on specific military projects, and are covertly threatened with termination of Pentagon support should they refuse."[12] (This implies that such scientists want to have Pentagon support in the first place.) Replying to the charge, Alexander J. Glass of the Naval Research Laboratory said: "This is a serious charge and, if true, it should be documented. If it is not true, the charge should quickly be retracted."[13] Professor Phillips did neither.

Professor Phillips prefers that all federal funds for academic research be channelled exclusively through the National Science Foundation, which may be a very good idea. But is he aware that the NSF, under existing legislation, is "authorized and directed," when the Secretary of Defense so requests, "to initiate and support specific scientific research activities in connection with matters relating to

---

11. *New York Times*, 5 May 1968, p. E-15.
12. Ibid., 9 June 1968, p. E-15.
13. Ibid., 23 June 1968, p. E-15.

national defense''? Does he know what the Defense Secretary may transfer funds for such research to the Foundation and that when he does so, he may "establish such security requirements and safeguards, including restrictions with respect to access to information and property, as he deems necessary''?[14] Does Professor Phillips remember that it was the NSF, not the Pentagon, that almost succumbed to congressional pressures to take away its grants to Professor Stephen Smale of the University of California at Berkeley? Smale is a world-renowned mathematician who criticized America's intervention in Vietnam at a mathematics meeting in Moscow in 1966.[15] Does Professor Phillips also know that it is the National Institutes of Health that has been placing distinguished scientists on blacklists, including Professor Salvador E. Luria of MIT, who won the Nobel Prize for Medicine in 1969?[16]

If scientists disagree so diametrically about the role of the Pentagon in funding academic research, is it any wonder that congressmen and laymen are so confused and concerned? And is that confusion or concern in any way lessened when prominent university researchers defend the positive outputs of *classified* research? Discussing and quoting academicians who make "The Case for Secret Research," *Time* magazine wrote:

> Stanford Electronics Laboratories Director William R. Rambo says that the irritating secrecy provisions are "a small price to pay" to stay on top of recent developments in his field. "To cut us off from classified research is to cut us off from the state of the art," says Michigan's Electrical Engineering Chairman Hansford W. Farris.
>
> Stanford Electrical Engineer Oswald Garrison Villard, Jr., who considers himself almost as ardent a pacifist as his father, the famed former editor of the *Nation*, has long been engaged in secret work related to rocket propulsion and guidance in order to keep abreast of his main scholarly interest: upper-atmosphere engineering. "To know what is important in this field, you have to be in on the classified aspect of it," he says.
>
> Despite the irritation of security and government red tape, many of the results of secret research eventually do get published, the professors insist. They also point out that most such projects have many nonclassified aspects that provide valuable training for Ph.D. candidates. At Michigan, for example, classified electronics research has produced at least 30 doctorates. A 26-acre antenna built at Stanford to help the U. S. learn how to detect enemy missile launches was used by Stanford Electrical Engineer Von R. Eshelman to bounce

---

14. 42 U.S.C. § 1862 (a) (3); § 1874 (b) (1).

15. Ibid., 18 August 1966, p. 22; 22 August 1966, p. 3; 27 August 1966, p. 1; and 18 October 1966, p. 44.

16. Ibid., 20 October 1969, p. 1.

the first radar signals off the sun. Classified research at Michigan
helped Emmett N. Leith develop the new science of holography . . .
which uses laser light to produce three-dimensional images. . . .
Says Leith: "The idea that you can close yourself off to these programs is pure ignorance."[17]

That the Vietnam War fuels the research debate among the professors and between them and the Pentagon is both obvious and
understandable. But it fuddles it, too. For example, early in 1968 Harvard's esteemed chemistry professor, Dr. George B. Kistiakowsky, who
was once science advisor to President Eisenhower, stopped advising
the Defense Department reportedly in protest over American policies
in Vietnam. Then, several months later, he complained in a letter to
Senator Fulbright about the "profound estrangement" between the
academic and defense communities. Kistiakowsky complained that
in the preceding five years the preeminent place held by university
scholars on the various Pentagon science advisory boards had been
taken over by "professional military scientists and those in the aero-
space industry and think tanks."[18]

For purposes of this discussion it isn't really very important that
defense officials rebutted that 45 percent of the members and three
of the four chairmen of the four most important boards were professors. What is important is that Professor Kistiakowsky ignored the
rebuttal and tried to have it both ways. How can he logically stop
consulting with the Defense Department—setting an influential example for others—and then complain that the Department was using
fewer university consultants, which the Department denied? The peda-
gogic value of this episode may really lie in what it tells us about
professors, not as scholars and scientists, but as people. For in matters of emotion and politics, it seems, they are just like everybody
else, if not more so.

This may be truest among social scientists, who are not and cannot be as objective as other scientists claim to be. This is why the
question of military funding and influence is particularly important in
these disciplines, which by definition study people. And people, including those who study other people, do have values, which they
frequently express and act out.

In June 1965, the existence of Project Camelot reached the headlines of the nation's press. A completely unclassified but army-spon-
sored social science research project, it "was designed to study the
political, economic, and social preconditions of instability and potential Communist usurpation of power in several developing coun-

---

17. 10 November 1967, pp. 55–56. Reprinted by permission from *Time, The Weekly
Newsmagazine,* Copyright Time Inc. 1967.
18. *New York Times,* 21 May 1968, p. 3; 2 June 1968, p. 61.

tries."[19] This it was to do with the help of the Special Operations Research Office of American University and leading social science consultants from other universities. Subsequently cancelled, it became a *cause célèbre* because it caused strong reactions from the White House, the universities, and members of Congress, in-fighting and jealousies between the Defense Department and other parts of the federal bureaucracy—particularly the State Department—and the anger of at least one foreign government, that of Chile.

Two political scientists who in the aftermath of Camelot argued the need—indeed the duty—of university social scientists to consult with and accept research support from the Defense Department are Professors Alfred de Grazia of Columbia University and Ithiel de Sola Pool of the Massachusetts Institute of Technology. One of de Grazia's responses to the negative reactions to Camelot was to ask his colleagues in an editorial in *American Behavioral Scientist:*

1. Is it not true that since 1940, the army, navy and air force have contributed incomparably more to the development of the pure and applied human sciences than the Department of State?

2. Is it not true that the State Department might on dozens of occasions have sought much more extensive research and intelligence facilities than it has actually sought or applied?

3. Is it not reasonable that the armed forces mission in respect to insurgency should include research on areas where revolution might occur?

4. Are Cuba and Santo Domingo, Lebanon and Vietnam and other cases too, going to stand as historical proof that the army can send men in to be killed but cannot help anyone go in *to forestall by preventive understanding the occasion of killing?*[20]

Pool describes the social sciences as "the new humanities of the twentieth century." He believes that the "only hope for humane government in the future is through the extensive use of the social sciences by government,"[21] both the popular agencies of government as well as the unpopular. "Everybody," he says,

likes the Department of Agriculture. It helps farmers and that is a good thing. Nobody objects to social scientists making their contributions to agricultural extension programs. Everybody likes the Department of Labor and would agree that if we could introduce better

---

19. U.S., Congress, House of Representatives, *Technical Information for Congress: Report to the Subcommittee on Science, Research, and Development of the Committee on Science and Astronautics*, Serial A. 91st Cong., 1st Sess. (Washington, D.C., Government Printing Office, 1969), p. 126. Italics mine. Chapter 6 of this report, prepared by the Library of Congress, is the most complete discussion of the Camelot episode that I have seen in the literature.

20. Quoted in ibid., pp. 140–141.

21. Ithiel de Sola Pool, "The Necessity for Social Scientists Doing Research for Governments," *Background* (since renamed *International Studies Quarterly*) 10 (August 1966), p. 111. Reprinted by permission.

human relations, better mediation, etc., it would be a good thing. Nobody objects to social scientists making contributions of that sort. Everybody among liberals likes AID [the Agency for International Development] and I am glad they do, because I can think of no more important program in the world today. Nobody objects to social scientists making their contribution to trying to figure out how to raise living standards in the developing countries around the world. But I do not want to make such easy cases. I want to make the hard case. I want to make the case that agencies like the [Defense Department], the FBI, or prisons, or the CIA need social scientists just as much as do the agencies that everybody likes.[22]

And he went on to make the hard case.

Professors de Grazia and Pool both noted that the State Department engages in and supports very little foreign areas studies research. They are thus in agreement with those of their critics who deplore that so much of this kind of research is done instead by CIA and DOD. Pool even goes so far as to suggest that one division of the Department of State be given a $10 million annual appropriation, an astronomical amount by present practice.

Although Tables 16 and 17 show clearly how tiny the State Department's research budget is in comparison with that of other federal agencies, they do not tell the whole story. The Department lacks a large domestic constituency—its "constituents" are, after all, foreign people and places—and because of this it always has difficulty getting its budgets through Congress. A vicious cycle operates here: since State Department budgets are hard to get through Congress, the Department has expectations of nonsupport. Having expectations of nonsupport, it often fails to ask for certain items in its budgets, such as research funds, that it really needs. Not asking for them, it doesn't get them, or it fares less well on these items in the budgetary competition with other agencies. And if it neither requests nor receives certain things, the Congress and the public in time begins to feel that it doesn't really need them to do their job properly.

But there is another factor. Many, if not most, senior Foreign Service officers feel that there is only one way to learn anything about foreign policy and international relations. That way is the long apprenticeship of diplomacy. If they respect any scholarly disciplines, they respect law, history, and languages the most. As Professor Gabriel Almond, a former president of the American Political Science Association, has phrased it:

I think the Department of State has a record of on the whole being unduly skeptical and unduly slow in stimulating and in carrying on

---

22. Ibid., p. 113. Reprinted by permission of International Studies Association.

TABLE 16

Federal Obligations for Social and Behavioral Research
on Foreign Areas and International Affairs

Agency	Fiscal Year 1967	
	Internal breakdown	*Total*
Agency for International Development:		
Central research	$4,451,922	
Regional bureaus	917,000	
		$5,368,922
Department of Agriculture		525,062
Arms Control and Disarmament Agency: Social, economic, and behavioral sciences		985,286
Department of Defense:		
Army	$4,853,005	
Navy	331,762	
Air Force	1,946,289	
Advanced Research Projects Agency (ARPA)	3,937,000	
International security affairs	1,947,632	
Systems analysis (Office of Secretary of Defense)	90,337	
		13,106,025
Department of Health, Education, and Welfare:		
Office of Education	$1,942,789	
Public Health Service	3,418,890	
Social and Rehabilitational Service	4,742,691	
		10,104,370
Executive Office of the President: National Council on Marine Resources and Engineering Development		561,477
National Endowment for the Humanities:		
Division of Fellowships and Stipends	$506,250	
Division of Research and Publications	386,190	
		892,440
National Science Foundation:		
Social Science Division	$5,579,850	
Economic and Manpower Studies	107,000	
		5,686,850
Peace Corps		292,829
Smithsonian Institution		920,231
Department of State:		
External research	$125,000	
International educational and cultural exchange program:		
American research scholars	745,790	
Assistance to centers for research and study abroad	480,889	
		1,351,679
U.S. Information Agency		537,887
Miscellaneous programs		280,895
Total		40,613,953

Source: U.S., Congress, *Technical Information for Congress: Report to the Subcommittee on Science, Research, and Development of the Committee on Science and Astronautics,* p. 127.

TABLE 17

Federal Funds for Psychological and Social Science Research
for Selected Agencies
(in millions of dollars)

	1961		1962	
	Psychological sciences	*Social sciences*	*Psychological sciences*	*Social sciences*
Total, all agencies	50.655	44.405	56.072	61.953
Department of Defense	17.177	0.215	15.113	0.203
Department of State	—	0.190	—	6.808
AID	—	0.190	—	6.808
Peace Corps	—	—	—	—
Arms Control & Disarmament	—	—	0.10	0.161

	1963		1964	
	Psychological sciences	*Social sciences*	*Psychological sciences*	*Social sciences*
Total, all agencies	72.4	79.9	96.3	102.7
Department of Defense	19.864	3.808	31.109	5.665
Department of State	—	1.699	0.130	3.817
AID	—	1.556	0.130	3.699
Peace Corps	—	—	0.325	0.230
Arms Control & Disarmament	0.355	2.069	—	1.359

	1965		1966	
	Psychological sciences	*Social sciences*	*Psychological sciences*	*Social sciences*
Total, all agencies	103.5	127.4	100.3	165.6
Department of Defense	21.321	4.886	21.7	8.4
Department of State	—	3.387	—	1.5
AID	—	3.262	—	1.5
Peace Corps	0.352	0.238	0.4	0.2
Arms Control & Disarmament	—	1.610	3.2	1.9

	1967		1968	
	Psychological sciences	*Social sciences*	*Psychological sciences*	*Social sciences*
Total, all agencies	107.3	177.6	124.4	209.3
Department of Defense	21.8	9.1	25.747	8.684
Department of State	—	1.7	—	1.025
AID	—	1.6	—	0.400
Peace Corps	0.18	0.39	0.125	0.375
Arms Control & Disarmament	0.034	1.605	0.190	2.083

Source: U.S., Congress, *Technical Information for Congress: Report to the Subcommittee on Science, Research, and Development of the Committee on Science and Astronautics*, p. 130.

social science research that has a direct bearing on the foreign policy interests of the United States. They are a conservative, humanistic institution, dominated by a foreign service which is trained largely in the law, in history, in the humanistic disciplines. They believe in making policy through some kind of intuitive and antenna-like process, which enables them to estimate what the prospects of this and that are in this or the other country.

I believe they are a backward agency, as far as their relationship to science is concerned.

. . . I wish the Department of State was more familiar, more receptive to some of the possibilities of social sciences than it now is. I think it has a real handicap in bringing to bear . . . , which could only come out of some change, it seems to me, in the fundamental culture of the Department of State.[23]

The military has no such handicap, or it has it to a much lesser degree. As the Science Policy Research Division of the Library of Congress reported to Congress after the Camelot Episode:

Although many Members of Congress had reservations about military research in social science questions abroad, and about the absence of coordination of such research by the Department of State, they discovered that the military initiative in this field was a natural consequence of the ability, no less than the need, of the Department of Defense to conduct such research. . . .[24]

The Library of Congress also said:

Although military sponsorship of social science research encountered little explicit endorsement and much criticism, it was also found hard to replace: Both strategic and tactical planning needed to be based on the kind of factual and conceptual inputs that the social sciences *alone* can provide.[25]

Congress and the public at large will and should continue to monitor and criticize the military role in American research, especially on American campuses. But they have an obligation to do this with as much logic, objectivity, and knowledge as is humanly possible.

When Senator Fulbright says that the universities provide the government with politically useful knowledge in return for badly needed funds does he mean that such army firsts—whether done by or for the army—as water chlorination, the discovery of the cause

23. Quoted in U.S., Congress, *Technical Information for Congress*, pp. 150–151.
24. Ibid., p. 127.
25. Ibid., pp. 159–160. [Italics mine.]

and cure of beriberi, the development of anthrax vaccine, and of a means of controlling the boll weevil in his native Arkansas are "political" rather than "scientific" achievements? Was he upset to learn that Walter Reed was an army surgeon and head of the army's Yellow Fever Commission when he proved that the transmitter of that dread disease was the *Aedes aegypti* mosquito? Does he consider that nothing of any scientific value derives from the navy's long-time interest in and support of university research in oceanography, navigation, and polar exploration? And is he trying to say that the air force's work in aero-space medicine is largely political?

When he criticizes, as he rightly should, the spectacle of (at least some) university administrators and researchers hungering after government contracts, and orienting their proposals to what they think the government wants, shouldn't he also mention that they do much the same kind of marketeering with the great private foundations? The latter have very definite, publicly announced, views about what they will and will not fund; rare is the researcher eager to make or keep a reputation who can prudently afford to ignore these ideas. Foundations are eager to support urban studies, for instance, and have encouraged young men to apply for grants in that field. But what of the young scholar who really isn't interested in urban studies and can't get a grant, or of the one who deliberately "pitches" his proposal in that direction just to get a grant?

This problem exists—in and out of government—even in the most nonpolitical and nonmilitary of disciplines. If the National Science Foundation is thinking physics this year, then the chemists are going to have a hard time of it. If the National Institutes of Health are on a heart "kick" this year, what does this do to the diabetes specialists? Or what about the professor of English who really loves Elizabethan drama but turns instead to linguistic analysis because he's heard that this is where the money is? And what about the poor fellow in Sumerian archaeology, for instance, who may not be able to apply to anyone for a grant?

Some very nonpolitical and nontechnological research projects have been funded by the Defense Department, among them "The Decline in Paternalism among Peruvian and Japanese Laborers"[26] and Mark Zborowski's and Elizabeth Herzog's *Life Is with People*, which is the best anthropological study of the culture of the East European Jewish *shtetl*. The latter book grew out of an Office of Naval Research grant to Professor Ruth Benedict's Research in Contemporary Cultures project at Columbia University.[27]

---

26. *New York Times*, 12 August 1969, p. 15.
27. Glick, *Peaceful Conflict*, p. 58.

Some people decry government support of such "impractical" research, or if they accept the need for it, they wonder why it must be paid for by the military. In truth, it need not be. But, as I have tried to show, which agency sponsors a particular piece of work is often a function of budgetary allocations by Congress. Furthermore, we can't always know if, when, and where a particular bit of research will have important value for peace or war. "The basic research that made the atomic bomb possible was all done in universities, without military support, and was as pure and untainted as you can imagine."[28]

In his book *A Long Row of Candles*, C. L. Sulzberger relates this anecdote:

> In early 1940 I visited General Weygand's *Armée du Levant* and, among the exuberant Spahis, Goumiers, and Légionnaires I noted hundreds of slant-eyed little Vietnamese, carrying stretchers or waiting on table. "Why," I asked, "are all the Annamites service troops?"
>
> The answer: "They can't fight." (Yes, the Vietnamese!)[29]

Would the French and then the Americans, I have often wondered, have wandered into their weary military confrontation with the North Vietnamese if they had first sought and received solid insights from university scholars specializing in the history, psychology, anthropology, sociology, and fighting capabilities of the Vietnamese?

As to the confrontation between the professors and the Pentagon, there are really only two main issues. The first is the "use [that] is made of knowledge (science) and skills (technology) and this is a more legitimate question than who sponsored discovery of the knowledge in the first place."[30] The second is the possibly corrupting influence of government money on the objectivity of university scholars. If they truly feel that all money corrupts but military money corrupts most corruptly, then let professors who consult to the Defense Department do so without fee, if not frequently then regularly. After all, university people are not above suggesting to members of the legal and medical professions that they provide free service under compelling national and social circumstances. Why don't we do the same?

University scholars are not nearly as objective as they think they are, but by training and tradition they are usually less subjective than their counterparts in industry and government. If because of Vietnam or for other reasons academia refuses to bring its powerful prestige and knowledge to bear on government and military programs and policies,

28. According to an unnamed government official quoted in the *New York Times*, 2 June 1968, p. 61.

29. C. L. Sulzberger, *A Long Row of Candles* (New York: Macmillan, 1969), p. xiv.

30. This is a paraphrase of the view of Dr. Donald Hornig, former science advisor to President Johnson, as stated in the *New York Times*, 2 June 1968, p. 61.

it will only force the armed services to set up more laboratory complexes of their own or to give huge new contracts to aero-space and other corporations. The result would be precisely opposite to the one desired by the student and faculty dissenters—a strengthening of the military-industrial complex and a diminution in the capacity of university scientists to exert any useful influence in the shaping of public policy on military matters.[31]

Even professors must realize that war and peace are too important to be left alone to the generals of the Pentagon.

---

31. Ibid., 4 June 1969, p. 40.

7

ROTC:
*From Riot to Reason**

Only a limited number of societies have been able to control their military by democratic political institutions. To achieve such control, the military cannot be isolated from society.[1]

As does any other citizen, an American college student has a perfect right to his own psychological, philosophical, political, practical, and purely personal and private reasons for adopting positions on public issues. If one of the positions he choses to adopt is to be against all wars or just the Vietnam War, to be against all armies or just the American army, then he also has a perfect right not to care a tinker's dam about how and where these armies get their officers. (Unless, of course, the officer selection process impinges itself on him directly and immediately through such means as military conscription or a compulsory Reserve Officers Training Corps program on his campus.)

If the student in question is either a selective or a consistent pacifist, he can always argue that if you do away with armies and

*Reprinted with permission from *Air Force/Space Digest*, official journal of the Air Force Association, 1750 Pennsylvania Ave., N.W.; Washington, D.C. 20006.
1. Roger Little, "Basic Education and Youth Socialization in the Armed Forces," *American Journal of Orthopsychiatry*, 38 (July 1968), p. 875.

their need to deter or engage in any kind of war for any kind of reason, you don't need any kind of officers. And if you therefore don't need an officer corps, then "Presto!," as the magician would say, you needn't concern yourself with such problems in a democracy as guarding against Prussianism, or the Garrison State, or the Military Mind, or the Closed Military Caste, or even the hallowed American principle of Civilian Control of the Military. There just won't be any military officers for civilians to have to fear and control.

In such a frame of mind, a student, as well as a nonstudent, can hardly be expected to be impressed by John Milton's view: "I call therefore a complete and generous education that which fits a man to perform justly, skillfully, and magnanimously all the offices, both public and private, of peace and war."[2] That student or nonstudent would certainly reject Samuel P. Huntington's justification for the broadest possible liberal education for the professional military officer, especially in a democracy:

> The military skill requires a broad background of general culture for its mastery. . . . Just as law at its borders merges into history, politics, economics, sociology, and psychology, so also does the military skill. Even more, military knowledge also has frontiers on the natural sciences of chemistry, physics and biology. To understand his trade properly, the officer must have some idea of its relation to these other fields and the ways in which these other areas of knowledge may contribute to his own purposes. In addition, he cannot really develop his analytical skill, insight, imagination, and judgement if he is trained simply in vocational duties. The abilities and habits of mind which he requires within his professional field can in large part be acquired only through the broader avenues of learning outside his profession. The fact that, like the lawyer and the physician, he is continuously dealing with human beings requires him to have the deeper understanding of human attitudes, motivations, and behavior which a liberal education stimulates. Just as a general education has become the prerequisite for entry into the professions of law and medicine, it is now also almost universally recognized as a desirable qualification for the professional officer.[3]

But what if the student or nonstudent has concluded—be he under 30, over 30, or exactly 30 years of age—that some kind of military establishment is still required in America, if only temporarily? He may

---

2. Quoted in U.S., Department of Defense, Office of the Assistant Secretary of Defense for Manpower and Reserve Affairs, *Report of the Special Committee on ROTC to the Secretary of Defense* (Washington, D.C.: 22 September 1969), pp. 8–9.

3. Samuel P. Huntington, *The Soldier and the State* (New York: Vintage Books, 1957), p. 14. © 1957 by The Belknap Press of Harvard University Press. Reprinted by permission.

even have come to that conclusion out of knowledge, as well as feeling, and with the sincerest conviction and the greatest unhappiness. He may believe that we need a more democratically responsive army, a smaller army, a less armed army, a cheaper army, a less internationally involved army, perhaps an all-volunteer army, and an army that has no business being or staying in Vietnam—but an army nonetheless. Then, if he really is a concerned citizen on or off the campus, he has to care, and care honestly, about how and where and at what cost we get our officers.

This latter kind of person must have an additional concern as well. He also has to care about the kind of human beings these military officers are or should be in a democracy. Milton and Huntington aside, while a case can be made for a direct relationship between a good education and good soldiering, such a relationship is not always present or necessary. Even where it exists, there is no automatic guarantee that out of it will come a well-educated and militarily competent officer who is *also* grounded in democratic tradition. Both present-day Israeli officers and German officers under Bismarck and Hitler know (or knew) how to fight well. Yet very few Israeli officers have had a university or military academy education and many, if not most, German officers did. The first live in and are firmly controlled by a democratic society; the second did not live in such a society and were certainly never controlled by it.

Thus, the really basic question here is: "Even if you grant that the best kind of officer in a democracy should have a liberal education, what is the best method of giving it to him and where is the best place for him to get it?"

The United States gets its active duty officers from several main sources. We have the four service academies: the Military Academy at West Point, the Naval Academy at Annapolis, the Air Force Academy at Colorado Springs, and the Coast Guard Academy at New London, Connecticut. We have the Officer Candidate Schools (OCS) and the Officer Training Schools (OTS). We have direct commissions into the services for professionally trained people such as physicians, psychologists, veterinarians, nurses, dentists, lawyers, chaplains, and others. We have some battlefield commissions of enlisted men into the officer ranks during wartime. In the case of the Marine Corps, we have the so-called Platoon Leaders Course. And we have the ROTC, from which most of our officers come.

As of September 1969, there were ROTC programs operating on 353 college and university campuses: the army had units on 283 campuses, the navy on 54, and the air force on 174. From 1968 to 1969 the army commissioned 16,415 new second lieutenants from its 150,982 ROTC cadets, compared to only 8,549 from OCS and 763 from West Point.[4] In November 1968, 10,760 midshipmen were in NROTC. From mid-1968 to mid-1969 "1,885 officers were commissioned to the fleet and 155 to the United States Marine Corps [which is part of the navy]. Slightly over 1,000 were commissioned in the regular navy, 300 more than from the . . . Naval Academy."[5] As for the air force, it had 51,273 AFROTC cadets at the time and it commissioned 4,977 second lieutenants.[6] In short, more than 23,000 new officers entered the armed services via the ROTC route during this period.

Moreover, while the majority of general and flag officers in the uniformed services are military academy graduates, ROTC graduates are now more visible in this category, too. For example, in the 1968 fiscal year 154, or a shade less than 30 percent, of the army generals on active duty or on the promotion list to general officer ranks were from ROTC. These included 82 brigadier generals, 69 major generals, and 3 lieutenant generals (William B. Rosson, University of Oregon, class of 1940; F.C. Weyland, University of California, class of 1939; and William R. Peers, University of California at Los Angeles, class of 1937).[7]

As the figures above and Tables 18 to 20 show, so few American officers come from the military academies and so many from ROTC. Also, the cost to the nation of commissioning an academy graduate is so high, while that of commissioning an ROTC man is relatively low, as seen in Table 21.

TABLE 18

Sources of New Army Officers

Source	Ten-Year Average (Fiscal Years 1957 to 1966)		Fiscal Year 1967	
	Number	%	Number	%
Military Academy	485	3.2	561	1.3
ROTC	8,593	55.9	10,629	24.1
OCS	1,187	7.7	19,240	43.7
All others	5,094	33.2	13,656	30.9

Source: U.S., Army, *Fifth Annual ROTC/NDCC Conference, 5 to 8 September, 1967* (Fort Monroe, Virginia: Continental Army Command Headquarters, 1967), p. 56

Thus, both the university students and the military authorities are vitally interested in the future of ROTC, albeit each for different reasons. The students cannot ignore the Vietnam War, its impact on

4. U.S., Department of Defense, *Report of the Special Committee on ROTC*, pp. 10–11.

5. Ibid., p. 14.

6. Ibid., p. 15.

7. U.S., Army, "Army Reserve Officers Training Corps Fact Sheet" (1 April 1969), supplied by the Department of Military Science of Temple University.

TABLE 19

Naval Officers on Active Duty by
Program (30 June 1967)

Program	Number
Naval Academy	11,289
NROTC (regular)	6,505
NROTC (contract)	1,878
OCS	15,453

Source: Compiled from a letter from the Director, Management Information Support Division, by direction of the Chief of Navy Personnel, Bureau of Naval Personnel, 25 March 1968.

TABLE 20

Air Force Officers on Active Duty by Source
of Commission (31 December 1967)

Source	Number
Air Force Academy	6,346
AFROTC	41,031
OCS	7,563
OTS (Officer Training School)	25,957
Aviation Cadets	35,897
All others	19,873

Source: Compiled from a letter from the Directorate of Personnel Training and Education, Office of the Air Force Deputy Chief of Staff for Personnel, 13 March 1968.

TABLE 21

Cost of Commissioning in Various Service Programs
(Fiscal Year 1967)

	Army	Navy	Air Force
Academy	$48,697.00	$40,200	$50,933
ROTC:			
Regular	4,775.00[a]	11,201	6,000
Contract	—	7,186	—
Two-year scholarship	6,541.00	—	—
Four-year scholarship	8,307.00	—	—
OCS (officer candidate school)	8,646.70[b]	2,025	—[c]
ROC (reserve officers course)	—	1,820	—
OTS (officers training school)	—	—	2,900
AECP and OTS (airman education and commissioning program)	—	—	22,000

[a]Latest figures available, fiscal year 1966.
[b]Average cost of OCS training. Costs vary by branch from a maximum of $12,068 for a field artillery regular officer to a minimum of $6,373 for an infantry reserve officer.
[c]Phased out OCS program in 1964.

their lives, and the anti-ROTC sentiments of some of their peers, who in extreme cases will use intimidation or violence to "get those killers off the campus." Nor can the military ignore its dependence upon ROTC. The chief of the army's ROTC division considers its elimination "disastrous."[8] He and his colleagues are well aware that freshman enrollment in the program appears to be dropping all over the nation. A sample of 30 campuses taken in October 1969 showed this not only in Ivy League colleges such as Harvard and Columbia, but also at Mississippi State, Berkeley, Colorado, Nebraska, five colleges and universities in Oklahoma, Ohio State, the University of Mississippi, Indiana, and Michigan.[9]

There is another problem. While each of the three ROTCs produces both regular and reserve officers, has two- and four-year programs, engages in summer training away from the campus, has some on-campus drill and wearing of the uniform, and teaches military history and strategy, there are some disquieting differences among them that affect the current national debate about them. As a Special Committee on ROTC pointed out to Secretary of Defense Melvin R. Laird:

> The army wants mostly reserve officers from ROTC; the navy wants mostly regular officers from ROTC; and the air force wants rated career officers from ROTC. The navy wants an "immediately employable ensign"; the army and the air force send their new lieutenants to service schools before using them on jobs. The air force tends to favor a two-year plan; the army accepted it and the navy has discontinued it. The army has tended to keep a weekly drill period; both the other services rarely drill more than six or eight times a semester. The air force has long had a program with much study of civilian-military policy; the army and the navy have moved more slowly into these fields. The navy teaches a substantial amount of technical information; the army a smaller amount; and the air force relatively litte. The navy carries over the service academy practice of forbidding marriage before graduation of scholarship holders but the other two services do not. The navy requires a contract of non-scholarship holders in the first two years; the other services do not. The navy excludes certain majors for scholarship holders; the others do not.
>
> Some civilian educators [and many students] frequently wonder why the three services are so far apart. At times various advisory groups have suggested the same first year or the same basic two years for all, *only to be sharply criticized by all the services which value their independence highly,* and which do use the ROTC for somewhat different purposes.

---

8. Colonel Everette Stoutner, quoted in the *New York Times*, 19 April 1969, p. 19.

9. For exact figures, see ibid., 20 October 1969, pp. 1 and 13.

The Committee sees little reason for trying to force uniformity on the services, although it notes that other countries have managed to combine some portion of officer training of their services. *It is, however, deeply concerned when a practice of one service leads to academic criticism of all ROTC and perhaps the elimination of all ROTC from an institution.* The Committee suggests that all three services could afford to have the same rule regarding marriage of cadets; the same rules regarding scholarship holders and contracts; positive rules about course majors; and similar emphases on drill and wearing of the uniform.

Specific issues of differences between the services may be minor in themselves, but they can become important in their effect on all ROTC.[10]

How did the military—though in different ways and for different reasons—become so dependent upon ROTC?

Just as Americans have been uneasy about the role of an espionage agency in a democracy, they have always been confused, contradictory, and controversial about their professional officer corps. And their officers know it. They often quote this little stanza written by one of Marlborough's veterans several hundred years ago:

> God and the soldier, we adore
> In time of danger, not before:
> The danger passed and all things righted
> God is forgotten, and the soldier slighted.[11]

(If America's professional soldiers are sometimes embittered by the treatment they receive from their civilian brethren, they are apparently never lastingly so.)

From its earliest years as a republic, two military traditions have competed for public attention and acceptance in America. The first was "born in the thoughts of Washington and Hamilton [and it] called for a professional army, albeit a small one, with an extremely professional corps of officers. It was under this tradition that the West Point military academy was born." The second, "espoused by Jefferson and Jackson, placed all faith in the common man. It called for vast citizen armies raised in mass only in times of emergency."[12]

The great clash between these two traditions climaxed during the Civil War. West Point-trained officers, fighting on both sides, were

---

10. U.S., Department of Defense, *Report of the Special Committee on ROTC*, pp. 59–60. Italics mine.

11. In Russel B. Reynolds, *The Officer's Guide* (Harrisburg, Pennsylvania: Stackpole Books, 1969), p. 11.

12. Lieutenant Frederic C. Tasker, "ROTC and the University: Friends or Enemies?" (unpublished paper, n.d.), p. 4.

used to leading only regulars, and had problems adjusting their tactics to unskilled volunteers. They tried complicated tactics that their inexperienced troops couldn't follow. Both sides made many blunders in this way.[13]

It was precisely because the Civil War proved the need for more officers, who could also understand nonprofessional enlisted men and draftees—plus the traditional American reluctance to expand the military academies to any great degree—that Congressman Justin Morrill included provisions for offering military courses in his monumental Land Grant Act of 1862. As he phrased it when advocating the Act's passage: "Something of military education has been incorporated in the bill in consequence of the new conviction of its necessity forced . . . by the history of the past years."[14]

If the Morrill Act was the first great ROTC milestone, the second was the National Defense Act of 1916, which authorized ROTC units in roughly the form we know them today. It was from this Act that the first army ROTC units came in 1916, the first navy units in 1926, and the first air force units in 1946. The third milestone, the one that provides the present statutory basis for the Reserve Officers' Training Corps, was the ROTC Vitalization Act of 1964. There are at least three stipulations in this last Act that even the Defense Department admits fuel the more legitimate opposition to ROTC today. These are that "no unit may be established or maintained at an institution unless . . ."

1. the senior commissioned officer of the armed force concerned who is assigned to the program at that institution is given the academic rank of professor,
2. the institution fulfills the terms of its agreement with the secretary of the military department concerned; and
3. the institution adopts, as a part of its curriculum, a four-year course of military instruction or a two-year course of advanced training of military instruction, or both, which the secretary of the military department concerned prescribes and conducts.

They will in time be changed or eliminated altogether.

But one charge often made against the military today—namely, that they decide whether an ROTC program is compulsory—is simply not true. It has never been true. Neither the Morrill Act of 1862, the 1916 Act, nor the 1964 Act has ever made ROTC mandatory on any

---

13. Ibid.
14. Quoted in U.S., Department of Defense, *Report of the Special Committee on ROTC*, p. 8.
15. Quoted in ibid., p. 10.

campus. Where it has been compulsory, it was made so by state law or university regulation, usually for reasons of patriotism.

As early as November 1924 the secretary of war, in a letter to a Philadelphia lawyer, wrote:

> I am pleased to inform you that the National Defense Act does not make military training compulsory at any of the institutions which receive the benefits authorized by the Act. So far as the War Department is concerned, it is optional with the authorities of the school, college, or university whether military training shall be an elective or a compulsory course in the curriculum.[16]

As late as February 1950—before the Korean War and *long before* the Vietnam War—the National Council Against Conscription (which was also against ROTC) was fair enough to say that "some colleges with compulsory ROTC create the impression that it is the federal government and not the college that is responsible." Citing college catalogues and correspondence, the Council proved that among colleges that did this at the time were the Colorado School of Mines, the University of Alabama, the University of Nevada, the University of Hawaii, and the University of Maryland.[17]

Anti-ROTCism and draft resistance are old traditions in America. How many of today's students know about the bloody 1863 draft riots in New York City? They produced a thousand human casualties, many of them blacks and abolitionists, and property damage estimated between $1.5 and $2 million.[18] Similarly, how many students know of a report which an officer assigned to MIT wrote in 1893 about the troubles of one of his predecessors? In it he says that the man,

> after a most uncomfortable war with the school authorities, succeeded in introducing some theoretical work. In order to do this he had to . . . remove the bright buttons from the (cadet) uniform and substitute for them gutta-percha buttons, as it was thought that the "brass buttons" gave the Military Department an altogether too prominent appearance.[19]

In the 1950s, when they were supposed to be interested more in panty raids than in political and social issues, students at the College of the City of New York, and at Dartmouth heckled and threw eggs at ROTC cadets parading on their campuses. It was during this decade

---

16. Quoted in John M. Swomley, Jr., et al., *Militarism in Education* (Washington, D.C.: National Council Against Conscription, 1950), p. 24.

17. Ibid.

18. William Bridgewater and Seymour Kurtz, eds., *The Columbia Encyclopedia*, 3rd ed. (New York: Columbia University Press, 1963), p. 593.

19. Quoted in Tasker, "ROTC and the University," p. 5.

also that the National Council Against Conscription mounted a broadside against ROTC as well. One of their arguments was a quotation from an army general that "ROTC units appear to spoil a good college student and do not make a good soldier." Another was that "Military training in college leads to a belief in the inevitability of war." Still another dealt with "the influence of American ROTC on Japanese militarism," which it partly blamed for the invasion of Manchuria. And still another was that

> . . . the presence of high-ranking officers on college faculties . . . endangers student and faculty freedom. Antiwar and anticonscription speakers may thus be prevented from using college facilities, if only because the college president or dean does not want to offend the ROTC officers and men. Sometimes also academic freedom can be jeopardized by the problem which arises from the antiwar teaching of a professor coming in conflict with the views of ROTC officers.[20]

How ironic and inaccurate was this last fear! If anything, it is the other way around today. It is the pro-ROTC officers, students, and professors whose academic freedom and access to university facilities are sometimes endangered. And if we remember that military officers have been assigned to civilian college campuses for over a century now, then we must happily conclude that they have done a pretty poor job in "militarizing" the average American student or professor. But few people have noted this fact during the passion, pain, and polarization of the Vietnam War debate.

The reaction of American college campuses to ROTC has ranged from riot to reason with the balance coming to rest somewhere in between. It has included pitched battles and the sacking and burning of the Military Science building at the University of Puerto Rico, the barring of ROTC students from class by a University of Kansas mathematics professor—he later relented—and the following announcement of peaceful hearings in the student newspaper of Temple University:[21]

HEARING ON ROTC

> Persons or organizations who would like to present recommendations or comments on the future role of ROTC training at Temple should write Dr. Bob A. Hedges, chairman of the University Subcommittee to make recommendations on policy with respect to ROTC, for an appointment time during the subcommittee's hearings, to be held Friday, October 31, starting at 1:30. Address Dr. Hedges at the School of Business Administration, Temple University.

---

20. Swomley, *Militarism in Education*, the inside of the front cover and pp. 41–44.
21. *New York Times*, 8 November 1969, p. 5; 14 February 1968, p. 53; and *The Temple News*, 29 October 1969, p. 7.

Give the name of the person or organization requesting time, and both an address and telephone number for communications from the subcommittee.

Each presentation should be addressed to the following choices of policy, which the subcommittee is considering:

1.   Participation by Temple in the ROTC program recently approved by the secretary of defense.* (A copy of this program, which is rather similar to the present program at Temple, may be seen at the Office of Faculty Senate, 3C Conwell Hall.)

2.   ROTC with all its academic subject matter handled by standard academic departments.*

3.   Same as 2, plus academic supervision of all drill and other "non-academic" ROTC classes on campus.*

4.   ROTC on campus, an officially recognized, but purely extracurricular activity at the University.

5.   All connection between Temple and ROTC be terminated.

*The extent to which ROTC courses would count toward a degree would be determined by the faculty of each degree-granting unit of the University, as at present.

Like that other furious debate over professorial "war research" on the campus, the one over ROTC has several overlapping dimensions and protagonists. There are those who:

1. Want ROTC to continue pretty much as it is now.
2. Want it to be voluntary (or compulsory).
3. Want it to carry (or not to carry) some academic credit toward graduation, the amount to be determined by the faculty.
4. Want the faculty to play a greater role in fashioning the ROTC curriculum.
5. Want academic credit given for ROTC courses taught by the regularly appointed civilian faculty but none for those taught by the resident professor of military science and his staff.
6. Want all ROTC courses related to civilian academic disciplines to be taught only by the regular faculty (e.g., leadership by psychology professors, international relations by political science professors, defense and disarmament expenditures by economics professors, and military history by history professors).
7. Are willing to accept some form of ROTC on campus but only if there are no uniforms, drills, rifles, parades, and other symbols of "militarism."
8. Insist that purely military courses such as naval engineering or rifle practice be given at off-campus centers during the regular academic year and/or at military camps during the summers.
9. Insist that the military personnel assigned to an ROTC unit, if there is to be one, not be called "professors."

10. Believe that ROTC should be removed from a university campus because the officers assigned to it are not academically qualified and the courses they teach are not intellectual enough for a university.

11. Do (or do not) want the decision to keep, change, or remove ROTC from a particular campus to be in any way influenced by a secret referendum of the students of the university, who are, after all, the people most directly concerned.

12. Are against ROTC on any campus in any shape or form, for any reason whatever, and want it to be removed immediately if not sooner.

People in this last category are especially difficult to write for or to talk to. They don't listen. For them there is no middle ground between reform and removal. Since they see no moral or military need for ROTC, they also see no need to find and study facts and opinions, to look for and to eliminate weaknesses and errors on both sides, and to work for a democratic accommodation between the military and academia. Yet most of them say they greatly fear a Prussianization or militarization of American society.

This is the same group that is impressed the least and worried the most by serious and thoughtful suggestions for an accommodation, such as the following advice given to the secretary of defense by a panel, most of whose members and all of whose advisors are university people: "The Committee does not believe that academic credit should be given or asked for learning simple routine operations like drill." Furthermore, it said that one "college president recently gave to another the following advice for his military instructors which the Committee believes should be carefully considered:

> We would advise you to emphasize strongly to your military staff, as we have done here, that in working with the present-day college student, they will be dealing with a very unique, complex, and a very valuable commodity. . . . He has a great potential for leadership in almost any field you can name. If properly treated and intelligently guided, he will respond amazingly well. But he will not respond to needless harassment, to having his valuable time wasted on minutiae, to a martinet-type approach, to obvious incompetency. . . . Everything he is exposed to must be meaningful and purposeful with at least some transfer value to what must be treated as an individual person, not as a rank and file number.[22]

To the highly emotional opponent of ROTC, this kind of advice to the military is only abetting an evil. ROTC is an evil. Every good

---

22. U.S., Department of Defense, *Report of the Special Committee on ROTC*, p. 46.

scholar and student is presumably opposed to evil. Therefore, they must all support ROTC's immediate removal from the nation's colleges and universities.

But just how far do you carry this kind of argument and logic? If Armies are equal to War, which is always Evil, and if Universities are equal to Peace and are always Good, do you, in addition to cancelling ROTC on every campus, also prevent officers already in the military from taking any courses and degrees at our civilian universities? If you let them take the courses and degrees, won't you then still be putting the "peaceful" university at the service of the "war-making" military? And is the best alternative to such a situation to send military men only to military academies and service schools with largely military instructors so that they hardly ever interact with civilian professors during their military careers?

Now, I hate Satan just as much as the next fellow. However, I am not as sure as others are that I can always recognize him when I see him. And I have always believed that a bit of passionate advocacy is good for the soul, good for debate, and even good for scholarship. But when passion subdues fairness and fact, and when emotion slays reason and logic—as they have done on many campuses—then honest discussion, peaceful change, and good policy-making must be the first casualties.

It is one thing for someone to say that "I am against ROTC, and that's that!" Such a position may appear to others to represent a closed mind, but at least an honest one. However, it is quite another thing to use arguments against ROTC that are specious, weak in logic, and ignorant of facts and consequences.

It is certainly proper, for example, to question the intellectual content of ROTC courses and to oppose granting credit for those that are intellectually deficient. But if you do this, you should define what you mean by "intellectual," you should compare ROTC courses with other courses on campus whose intellectuality is also questionable (accounting? physical education? home economics? insurance?), and you should do your damnedest to bring *all* such questionable courses up to intellectual snuff.

Or let us consider the case of the student or faculty member who bases his objection to ROTC partly on the lack of proper academic credentials for the military officers who staff the courses. Certainly there are some outrageously bad and out-of-touch ROTC instructors on some of our campuses. But don't we have some pretty incompetent civilian professors, many with tenure, on some of our campuses? This is not a new problem for the universities nor for the military. In the late 19th century someone described an army officer assigned to MIT as: "Colonel __, antecedence and real occupation unknown. He held the reins (from 1880) until 1883, having become, I believe, too old to walk."[23]

But things and times have changed now. Universities have for years had much more flexibility with regard to ROTC appointments than they have chosen to exercise. How many people have ever seen a copy of the present standard contract between the army and a university that has an ROTC unit on its premises (see Figure 4)? How many administrators, faculty members, and students know of the contract's clause 3c, which states: "That no army officer shall be assigned to the Department of Military Science without prior approval of the authorities of this institution [i.e., the school, college, or university], and no army officer will be continued on duty after the authorities have requested his relief for cause"? How many universities have ever vetoed the projected assignment of an officer to ROTC for lack of academic qualifications or any other reason? How many have asked for the recall of an officer for lack of academic qualifications or any other reason? How many universities have exercised their right to insist that all professors of military science have Ph.D.s or master's degrees (and many military officers have them)? And most important of all, how many anti-ROTC students and professors who use the "union card argument" would really be willing to change their positions if the universities insisted on graduate-trained officers and if the military supplied them?

Furthermore, we are now living in the era—long overdue—of more student participation in university governance both by voice and vote. How many campus opponents of ROTC who cry out for the greatest possible degree of student participation in university decision-making would let the decision on whether and in what form to keep ROTC rest in the hands of a secret and binding student referendum? I know of one university where 35 percent of the seniors felt that ROTC should remain on campus with credit and 17 percent felt it should stay without credit. Yet, despite this 52 percent majority, a special student-faculty committee recommended 4 to 2 that the Corps be removed entirely from the campus.[24]

What we have now on many campuses is a political equation vis-à-vis ROTC that can be represented by the formula:

$$V + P + F + S + RO = C$$

where V = the Vietnam War, P = the Pentagon, F = the faculty, S = the students, RO = ROTC, and C = confrontation with the administration.

---

23. Quoted in Tasker, "ROTC and the University," p. 6.
24. The university is Temple. See *TEMPO: for the Temple Faculty*, 24 October 1969, p. 3; and *The Temple News*, 14 November 1969, p. 1.

What we should have is a situation on each campus that can be expressed as follows

$$V + Pf + Ff + Af + Sf + ROf + B = A \text{ or } RE$$

where V = the Vietnam War, Pf = a flexible Pentagon, Ff = a flexible faculty, Af = a flexible administration, Sf = a flexible student body, ROf = a flexible ROTC department, B = a secret student ballot on the issue, A = an accommodation, and RE = ROTC's removal by a democratically arrived at decision.

Whatever happens on any particular campus or group of campuses, the fact is that we have needed more officers than the military academies and OCS could produce before and during the Vietnam War, and we shall probably need them after that war even if our future military posture and commitments are drastically reduced. The fact is, too, that while some colleges are moving to banish ROTC, others are waiting to receive it, as indicated in Figure 5.

ROTC will remain in this country for some time, whatever its form and whatever its name. Do we, then, want to recruit all of our college-trained officers from only certain sections of the country, with only certain kinds of political and social views, and from only certain universities that, unjustly or not, do not have the reputation, prestige, and intellectual excellence of the institutions that have removed or will remove ROTC from their hallowed halls and lawns? Even if it were physically and economically possible for us to get all of our officers from the service academies, would we really want to do so?

I think not. Instead, like Michael Harrington, the author of *The Other America*, to whom we are indebted for painting a vivid portrait of poverty in the United States, I worry about the "inborn and conservative" education of most of our Academy-trained generals and admirals. As he does,

I hold no brief for the military, whether it is efficient or not and I would like to see a world in which it simply did not exist. But since that happy day is not exactly imminent, this country should worry a little more about how it picks the [military] men who hold the life and death of the planet in their hands.[25]

---

25. From his column in the *Philadelphia Bulletin*, 2 February 1969, sec. 2, p. 11.

FIGURE 4

Sample Application and Agreement for Establishment of Army Reserve Officer's Training Corps Unit

SUBJECT: Application for the Establishment of Army Reserve Officers' Training Corps Unit

THRU : (1) Commanding General, _____ United States Army,
 (2) Commanding General, United States Continental Army Command. Fort Monroe. Virginia 23351
TO : The Adjutant General, Department of the Army, Washington. D.C. 20315

APPLICATION

I _____
 (Name)

By direction of the governing authorities of _____
 (Name of Institution)

_____
 (Title)

hereby submit application for the establishment of a unit in the senior division of the Army Reserve Officers' Training Corps at this institution under the provisions of section 2102. Title 10, United States Code. Attached hereto is a catalog and a statement of particulars with reference to this institution.

AGREEMENT

1. Contingent upon the acceptance of the above application and conditioned upon the fulfillment of all promises enumerated in paragraph 2 following, the Secretary of the Army agrees as follows:

a. To establish and maintain a senior division unit of the Army Reserve Officers' Training Corps at the institution named in the foregoing application.

b. To assign such military personnel as he may deem necessary for the proper administration and conduct of the Army Reserve Officers' Training Corps program at this institution and to pay the statutory compensation to such personnel from Department of the Army appropriations.

c. To provide for use in the Army Reserve Officers' Training Corps program such available Government property as may be authorized by law and applicable tables of allowances, and to pay at the expense of the Government costs of transportation, drayage, packing, crating, handling and normal maintenance of such property, exclusive of costs including utilities, involved in the storage of such property at the institution.

d. To pay at the expense of the Government, subject to law and regulations. retainer pay at a prescribed rate to enrolled members of the Army Reserve Officers' Training Corps admitted to advanced training.

e. To arrange for the scheduling of military classes to make it equally convenient for students to participate in Army Reserve Officers' Training Corps as in other courses at the same educational level, and to include a representative of the Department of Military Science designated by the Professor of Military Science on all faculty committees whose recommendations would directly affect the Department of Military Science.

f. To appoint an officer of the institution as military property custodian who will be empowered to requisition, receive, stock and account for Government property issued to the institution and otherwise to transact matters pertaining thereto, for and in behalf of the institution, or to comply with provisions of the supplement to this agreement (DA Form 918a), if application is made for and the Army accepts responsibility for all Government property provided for military instruction at this institution.

g. To conform to the regulations of the Secretary of the Army relating to issue, care, use, safekeeping, turn-in and accounting for such Government property as may be issued to the institution.

h. To comply with the provisions of law and regulations of the Secretary of the Army pertaining to the furnishing of a bond to cover

e. To issue at the expense of the Government uniform clothing for enrolled members of the Army Reserve Officers' Training Corps, except that monetary allowances, at the prescribed rate or rates, may be paid in lieu of uniform clothing.

f. In providing financial assistance to specially selected members under the provisions of section 2107 of Title 10, United States Code, to arrange accounting procedures with the appropriate fiscal officer of the institution.

2. Contingent upon the acceptance of this application by the Secretary of the Army and conditioned upon the fulfillment of the promises enumerated in paragraph 1 above, the governing authorities of this institution agree as follows:

a. To establish a Department of Military Science as an integral academic and administrative department of the institution and to adopt as part of its curriculum ☐ (1) a four-year course of military instruction; ☐ (2) a two-year course of advanced training of military instruction; or ☐ (3) both of the above, which the Secretary of the Army will prescribe and conduct.

b. To require each student enrolled in any Army Reserve Officers' Training Corps course to devote the number of hours to military instruction prescribed by the Secretary of the Army.

c. To make available to the Department of Military Science the necessary classrooms, administrative offices, office equipment, storage space, and other required facilities in a fair and equitable manner in comparison with other departments of the institution.

d. To grant appropriate academic credit applicable toward graduation for successful completion of courses offered by the Department of Military Science.

the value of all Government property issued to the institution, except uniforms, expended articles, and supplies expended in operation, maintenance and instruction.

i. To produce a minimum of twenty-five officers each year.

j. To maintain an enrollment of one hundred in the basic course, when the basic course is maintained.

3. It is mutually understood and agreed as follows:

a. That this agreement shall become effective when the authorities of this institution have been notified officially that the Secretary of the Army has approved the establishment of an Army Reserve Officers' Training Corps unit on the date specified.

b. That this agreement may be terminated upon giving one academic year's notice of such intent by either party hereto.

c. That no Army officer shall be assigned to the Department of Military Science without prior approval of the authorities of this institution, and no Army officer will be continued on duty after the authorities have requested his relief for cause.

d. That the Secretary of the Army shall have the right at any time to relieve from duty any officer, warrant officer, or enlisted man of the Army assigned to the institution.

4. The authorities of this institution understand that the law requires that no unit may be established or maintained at an institution unless the senior commissioned officer assigned to the institution is given the rank of professor.

5. This agreement supersedes all existing agreements between the Department of the Army and the institution pertaining to this matter.

FOR THE INSTITUTION	
SIGNATURE	DATE
TYPED NAME AND TITLE	

FOR THE SECRETARY OF THE ARMY	
SIGNATURE	DATE
TYPED NAME AND TITLE	

FIGURE 5
College and Universities Adding ROTC Units
(1968 to 1970)

State College of Arkansas, Conway

Arkansas A.M. and N., Pine Bluff

West Illinois University, Macomb

Morehead State University, Kentucky

Central Missouri State College, Warrensburgh

Rider College, Trenton, New Jersey

Eastern New Mexico University, Portales

St. John's University, Jamaica, New York

Stephen F. Austin State College, Nacogdoches, Texas

Brigham Young University, Provo, Utah

Wisconsin State University, at Oshkosh and Stevens Point

University of South Alabama, Mobile

Southeastern Louisiana College, Hammond

Appalachian State University, Boone, North Carolina

Rochester Institute of Technology, Rochester, New York

Old Dominion College, Norfolk, Virginia

Wisconsin State University, Whitewater

Northern Illinois University, Dekalb

Northern Michigan University, Marquette

Long Island University, Greenvale, New York

Central State College, Edmond, Oklahoma

Northeast Missouri State College, Kirksville

Francis T. Nichols State College, Thibodaux, Louisiana

Florida Institute of Technology, Melbourne

Southern Colorado State College, Pueblo

Kearney State College, Kearney, Nebraska

Jackson State College, Jackson, Mississippi

Virginis Commonwealth University, Richmond

Boise College at Boise, Idaho

Source: *New York Times*, 4 February 1969, p. 9.

8

Should We Eliminate
or Merge
Our Military Academies?*

In a time of rising domestic antimilitarism, there is surprisingly little civilian, and especially college, criticism of America's military academies. Perhaps after using so much of their energy against ROTC and on-campus military recruiters, our professors and students don't have much left to direct against Annapolis, Colorado Springs, and West Point, whence come our highest uniformed defense officials.

There is something even more surprising. When Americans do criticize their military academies, the harshest critics are usually military men—many of them academy alumni—and not civilians. For example, in 1968 a Special Subcommittee on Service Academies reported to its parent body, the House Armed Services Committee: "On the basis of this careful review, the subcommittee is pleased to report that in its considered judgment the three service academies are being operated and administered in complete accordance with existing law and are fulfilling, in a satisfactory manner, the mission assigned them by the Congress."[1] The Subcommittee's report of nearly a thousand

---

*A version of this chapter appears in the January 1971 issue of *Foreign Service Journal*, and is included here with permission.

1. U.S., Congress, *Administration of the Service Academies*, p. 10,224b. Though this document is heavily biased in favor of the military, it contains much recent and valuable statistical data.

pages is replete with such reassurances to the testifying military personnel as: "I am not asking these questions in an unfriendly sense whatsoever . . ."; or "Because on this committee are men who have served a long time in the service, who have been dedicated to the best interests of the military, and who have proven themselves time and time again the best friends a man in uniform had . . ."; or

> Now, may I say this, and just in a brief capsule form, that our objective—we are not coming to the Academy, the Naval Academy, as well as the other two sister Academies, with a chip on our shoulder. We are coming in the most cooperative spirit we can muster. We both want to attain the same goal. We want to know exactly what is going on. And as an indication of our attitude there will not be any public hearings during the inquiry of this committee.[2]

By contrast, the military critics of the military academies have been far less generous and solicitous. Well over a century ago, General John A. ("Black Jack") Logan, who was one of the North's few volunteer general officers in the Civil War, had this to say about the United States Military Academy and its products:

> West Point has for years taken possession of the military interests of the government and has conducted those interests as the sole property of the select circle which by the decrees of West Point has been constituted the only true exponent of the art of war upon the American continent.[3]

The Air Force Academy, the nation's newest one, got one of its biggest blasts from Lieutenant Colonel Charles Konigsburg in a letter he wrote in 1967 to Congressman F. Edward Hébert, chairman of the Special Subcommittee on Service Academies. In his letter the colonel charged, among other things:

> First, . . . no young man, however capable and intelligent, can handle the total academy program in the proper manner and spirit. . . . [The] average cadet has an academic schedule and workload in excess of that required at the best colleges. . . . To the academic program, which demands 75 to 80 percent of the cadet's time and preoccupation, *add* a mandatory military training program, a required athletic program, cadet squadron duties, and other requirements.
>
> [Second, if,] as most cadets soon come to understand, the object of the "game" (recognized and described by them as such) is to pursue the image of "instant academic excellence" in terms of its popular symbols (test scores, grades, extra courses, major programs,

---

2. Ibid., pp. 10,367, 10,758, and 10,895.

3. Quoted in Russell F. Weigley, *Towards an American Army* (New York: Columbia University Press, 1962), p. 134.

scholarships, postgraduate study, academic conference image-building, etc.) and not primarily to acquire substantive understanding of subject matter or to develop attitudes and habits of conscientious dedication to maximum effort in all assigned and related tasks—*then, why not cheat?*

[Third,] criticism has simply not been tolerated at the Academy, on the faculty. It is equated with "disloyalty" and "subversion." . . . The "mortal sin" at the Academy, one soon learns, is not in wrongs committed or overlooked: the mortal sin lies in raising questions about the situation, especially in talking outside of the family—as I am doing here.

[Fourth, one] who has served a tour of duty at the Air Force Academy under the original assumption that he would help to train the future "creative leadership" of the USAF is led to the following conclusion: that at the AF Academy it has been forgotten that its mission is to produce dedicated and enlightened young officers, not prospective candidates for scholarships and graduate schools or practitioners of academic gamesmanship. We ought surely to do whatever is necessary to enhance the intellectual caliber of our officer corps—in this I yield to no man!—but if it is scholars, etc. we want, let us send these fine young men to the best universities, give them military training during the summers, an active duty commitment afterward, for one-fourth the cost.[4]

And as for the Naval Academy, its most persistent critic, if not its most beloved graduate, is Vice Admiral Hyman G. Rickover, who has often spoken out about academic shortcomings at our civilian colleges as well. Testifying before Congress in 1968, he said: "Naval Academy midshipmen generally lack poise, self-confidence and maturity. They give the appearance of having these qualities, but it is a superficial appearance with little depth."[5] Admiral Rickover's unhappiness goes beyond Annapolis. He once said of *all* the academies:

No institution can depart too much from the norms of its particular society and function effectively as part of that society. The service academies have set themselves apart from their society. This has resulted in strains, and is one of the chief reasons why officers are not able to identify with the new forces which are exerting influence on the military. The academies should, as soon as possible, stop setting themselves up as a higher ethical society by the use of honor codes, etc. If they continue to do this they will inevitably broaden the gulf between the military and reality. . . . Senior officers at the academies . . . are so anxious to prove their own integrity and their ability to create a perfect society under their auspices that they forget their responsibilities to do all they can for the youth in their charge,

---

4. U.S., Congress, *Administration of the Service Academies*, pp. 10,898–10,899.
5. Quoted in *Philadelphia Bulletin*, 15 July 1968, p. 4.

to sacrifice themselves if need be for the youth. Instead, *they impose standards . . . which probably they themselves have never met* and which are not practicable in the services. Such standards are not set up by the colleges from which the army, navy, and air force draw by far the great majority of their officers, *nor are they used among officers in the services themselves.*[6]

If these charges against the military academies are even only partly true, they are serious enough to raise some questions. Do we *really* need our military academies? Or do we just have them because we have them and because other countries have them? Do we keep them at great federal cost, only because of history, habit, tradition, and the political unthinkability of doing away with them? Or do we keep them because of *proven* military necessity in the light of present-day methods of waging war and peace? Is the United States Marine Corps officer less of a fighting man than his colleagues in the other services because he usually is *not* an academy product, but a graduate of a civilian university and the Corps' Platoon Leaders Course? And if we cannot or should not do away with the academies, should we *merge* them into a single institution, at least at the lower levels of instruction?

Before we can answer any of these questions intelligently and affirmatively, we ought to compare the American practice with that of a foreign democratic country that maintains one of the finest fighting forces in the world and yet does not have a college-level military academy. We ought also to know something about American military academy drop-out figures and about officer production and retention figures from these academies. And we ought to compare these figures meaningfully with analogous figures for American officers who are not graduates of West Point, Annapolis, or Colorado Springs.

The foreign democratic country whose experience may have some transfer value for the United States is Israel. She has no military academies on the college level and no ROTC-type program at her civilian universities. This is so because most Israeli men are not permitted to enroll in college before they have completed their three-year tour of obligatory service, which starts at the age of 18. What the Israelis do have, for a small number of their future career officers in the unified Israel Defense Force, are two *pnimiot tzvaiot* (military boarding schools) at the high-school level. One is in the Tel-Aviv area—I visited it and interviewed its commandant in August 1968—and the other is

---

6. Quoted in J. Arthur Heise, *The Brass Factories* (Washington, D.C.: Public Affairs Press, 1969), pp. 184–85. Italics mine. This book is itself a highly critical appraisal of West Point, Annapolis, and Colorado Springs.

in the Haifa area. Here is how they work.[7]

Although they are called in Hebrew *military* boarding schools, they are really military civilian schools, and this is the important point. As Colonel Baruch Levy, the director of the school near Tel-Aviv, put it: "If the Army had decided to do so, it would have been very simple to get together some teachers and open our own separate school. But that is precisely what was not wanted." Instead, the cadets in the Tel-Aviv area attend classes in the mornings and early afternoons at the famous Herzliah High School in Tel-Aviv and those in the Haifa area do the same at the equally prestigious Reali High School in Haifa. They follow the regular curriculum and standards that the civilian boys and girls at these schools must follow, and while they are in class the cadets wear civilian garb. It is only after they are returned by bus to the *pnimia* at about 2 P.M., that the cadets change into uniforms and begin the military portion of their studies and training as well as their civilian homework. After four years at the *pnimia*, for which their parents pay 750 Israeli pounds yearly, the boys graduate with the rank of corporal and go on to Officers Training School. Leaving the *pnimia* with the lowly rank of corporal tells us something about the Israeli approach to officership and to the intended relationship between officers and men. An Israeli—even a military boarding school graduate—becomes an officer only by climbing the ranks from the bottom to the top. The road is from enlisted man to noncommissioned officer to regular or reserve officer, and for the talented and motivated, the road can be a rapid one.

In short, the whole purpose of not having a military academy as we know it and for making officers first serve in the enlisted or NCO ranks is to maintain and reinforce the "citizen's army" character of the Israel Defense Force. As one observer wrote in the *Jerusalem Post Weekly*: "The notion of having future officers—possibly even the Chief of Staff of the future—attend classes together with future professionals—and future housewives—is in itself a clear statement of this country's attitude toward 'militarism.' "

As for American military officers who come (or do not come) from the military academies, the plain fact is that West Point, Annapolis, and Colorado Springs just do not and cannot produce enough graduates, even if we were all satisfied with their education, their promise,

---

7. The following description is based on my visit and interview with Lieutenant Colonel Baruch Levy in Israel on 4 August 1968; Colonel Irving Heymont, "The Israeli Career Officer Corps," *Military Review* 48 (October 1968), 15; "Military Academy Graduates 14th Class," *Jerusalem Post*, 1 August 1968, p. 5; and a long and quite detailed feature article on the *pnimia* in the Tel-Aviv area, which appeared in the *Jerusalem Post Weekly*, 25 December 1967, p. 9.

and their performance. For economic, physical, and political reasons, the three academies are "not easily expanded or contracted to meet emergency expansion needs or to counter lessened needs."[8] In 1968, at the height of our involvement in Vietnam, the then Secretary of Defense Robert S. McNamara issued a statement to Congress projecting America's defense posture and needs for the fiscal years 1969 to 1973. Despite our heavy military manpower commitments and losses in Vietnam, McNamara talked about enlarging West Point's and Colorado Springs' enrollment to only 4,400 each, and keeping Annapolis' enrollment at about 4,100.[9]

Moreover, what the military calls "disenrollment" from the three academies is not low. If we look at the classes from 1958 to 1970, we find that the dropout rate for all reasons has ranged from 19.4 to 33.9 percent for the Military Academy, 22.3 to 35.7 percent for the Naval Academy, and 15.4 to 40.2 percent for the Air Force Academy.[10]

"But," some may say, "even if the academies' officer production figures are low, and their dropout rates are high, look at the higher retention rates of academy men after they are commissioned and look at the high percentage of academy graduates in the upper ranks of the services. Doesn't this prove their superior training and devotion?"

It does and it doesn't. As with other forms of fact, statistical data have to be compared and interpreted. At first glance, academy graduates do indeed appear to remain in the services for a much longer period than do other officers. But J. Arthur Heise argues that this is illusory.[11] It is not really the case, if we compare apples with apples rather than with pears. He contends that if we compare the departure rate of ROTC men who enter the services as *regular*, rather than reserve, officers, against the departure rate of academy graduates, who can only enter with regular commissions, we find that the differences in retention rates are very low for two out of the three services. He cites a 1964 study which showed that 23.7 percent of the West Pointers who entered the army between 1950 and 1960 resigned, compared to 24.5 percent of the ROTC-produced Distinguished Military Graduates (DMGs) who entered the Army with regular commissions during the same period. He says that in the air force the departure rate for the first three classes of the Air Force Academy was 27 percent, compared with a 37 percent rate for DMGs from AFROTC. Only in the navy does the NROTC-trained officer leave at a much

8. U.S., Department of Defense, *Report of the Special Committee on ROTC*, p. 19.

9. U.S., Department of Defense, *Statement by Secretary of Defense Robert S. Mc-Namara on the Fiscal Year 1969 to 1973 Defense Program and the 1969 Defense Budget* (Washington, D.C.: 22 January 1968), p. 180.

10. U.S., Congress, *Administration of the Service Academies*, p. 10,257.

11. Heise, *The Brass Factories*, pp. 157–61.

higher rate than his Annapolis counterpart. For the Naval Academy classes of 1959 to 1961, the rate averaged less than 30 percent; for *regular* NROTC men who had finished their obligated service, the departure rate during fiscal years 1959 to 1961 was 60 percent. As for more recent figures, the *New York Times* reported in October, 1970 that the retention rate for Army graduates of ROTC and OCS was 18.6 percent for fiscal year 1970, with a projected rate of 31.5 percent for fiscal year 1971. By way of comparison, the West Point rate for the class of 1963 was 24 percent.[12]

With regard to the argument that the academies prove their usefulness and are worth their cost if only because the vast majority of America's generals and admirals are academy graduates, two points can be made. First, academy graduates dominate the selection boards that choose the people to be promoted to these ranks, just as they favor "wearers of the old school tie" when they chose people for assignments to the prestigious senior service schools. Second, "the apparent lack of opportunity for advancement [to general and flag officer rank] may help to account for the lower retention rates of nonacademy personnel. The relationship might very well be circular: nonacademy people don't stay because they don't get promoted and they don't get promoted because they don't stay."[13] If nonacademy officers feel that they have a much lower chance of "making" general or admiral than their colleagues from the academies, why should they stay?

If there really isn't a great disparity in retention rates between academy and nonacademy officers; if the disparity would be even smaller if the nonacademy officers did not feel discriminated against in top promotions; if the cost of an academy education to the federal government is so high; if there is no evidence that academy officers perform better than other officers; and if we are truly worried about isolating our professional officer corps from civilian influences—then shouldn't we eliminate the academies altogether?

Perhaps we should, but we won't. For one thing, it seems highly unlikely that we can eliminate the military academies at a time when there is so much pressure from the colleges to eliminate ROTC as well. We can't do away with both of these sources of officer procurement, certainly not simultaneously. For another thing, history, tradition, nostalgia, the armed services, the veterans' organizations, the Congress, and the public would probably all combine to defeat any such move.

So if we can't eliminate West Point, Annapolis, and Colorado

---

12. *New York Times*, 26 October 1970, p. 40.
13. I am indebted for this point to Richard Smith, my former graduate research assistant and a student in my seminar on national defense politics.

Springs, should we then merge them into a single National Defense Academy?

There would be a great deal of good, I think, in an institution in which during the first two or three years the students would wear a single uniform—or no uniform—and would take common courses in both military and civilian subjects. There would be advantages to a learning situation that would deemphasize service rivalries and stress the interrelationship of air, sea, and land forces and doctrine, as well as the intimate connection between political and military factors in making and executing the nation's foreign and domestic policies. Perhaps people wanting to enter the State Department's Foreign Service, the United States Information Agency, the Agency for International Development, and the Central Intelligence Agency would also enroll in such a National Defense Academy. Perhaps such an institution would require a five-year program, during the last two years of which the students would opt for or "major in" the army, navy, or air force and transfer to the present Military Academy, Naval Academy, or Air Force Academy. At the very least, the first three years together might cause the students to think along wide *government* lines rather than along narrow, single *service* lines, as at present. And when some of these students become our future generals, admirals, and senior diplomats, these same three years of study might enhance that broad outlook that they will have to have to work well together in the best interests of the nation.

We ought at least to experiment with a National Defense Academy. If it fails, then all that we have lost is some money and time. But if it succeeds, we may gain something much more precious than money and time. We may gain a well-educated officer corps that is oriented toward the nation and the world rather than to themselves and their service. It is certainly worth a try.

9

Medical Civic Action:
A Policy Suggestion

Military men the world over love to use jargon, and the Americans are no exception. A current favorite is "military civic action," which the *cognoscenti* usually shorten to "civic action." Nobody is quite sure where the term originated, and as so much other military jargon, it has that nondescriptive quality that one often finds in the vocabulary of government generally. But it does have a meaning: In the United States the Joint Chiefs of Staff have defined it officially as "The use of preponderantly indigenous military forces on projects useful to the local population at all levels in such fields as education, training, public works, agriculture, transportation, communications, health, sanitation, and others contributing to economic and social development which would also serve to improve the standing of the military forces with the local population. (U.S. Forces may at times advise or engage in military civic actions in overseas areas.)"[1]

Both the definition and the thrust of civic action are directed to underdeveloped countries.[2] But even the most developed and demo-

___
1. U.S., Joint Chiefs of Staff, *Dictionary of United States Military Terms for Joint Usage*, JCS Pub. 1 (Washington, D.C.: Government Printing Office, 1964), pp. 90–91.

cratic of nations have pockets and periods of socioeconomic distress and transition. America is one of them, and I want to suggest a military medical civic action program for use *within* the United States. There is both precedent and need for it.

The most recent precedent occurred in 1965.[3] As part of Exercise Polar Strike, army Special Forces performed medical, dental, and veterinary civic action in Indian and Eskimo villages in Alaska in cooperation with the United States Public Health Service (USPHS) and the Alaska Department of Health and Welfare. Consultations among these three agencies before the Exercise produced a decision that army personnel would engage in:

1. Teaching natives basic first-aid procedures, and giving general hygiene and nutritional instruction based on current publications furnished by the USPHS.

2. Advising the village council, through the village Health Aide, concerning sanitation methods and techniques.

3. Teaching, advising, and helping village Health Aides in patient care.

4. Rendering medical and dental care within the capability of the detachment medics and the Civic Action Team.

5. Consulting USPHS area physicians and dentists concerning patient management.

6. Obtaining information on capabilities, limitations, and utilization of dogs; gathering information on zoonotic diseases that could affect troops and/or animals deployed to Alaska; and participating in recommended disease control and eradication civic action programs.

The order of priority for medical examination and treatment was: (1) school children, (2) preschool children and their mothers, (3) pregnant women, (4) people over 60, and (5) anyone else who needed medical or dental care. Emergencies were, of course, seen at the time they occurred. As for the training and preventive care programs, these were all within the guidelines already established by the state Health and Welfare Department and by the United States Public Health Service.

---

2. For the most comprehensive discussions of civic action as it is practiced worldwide, see Glick, *Peaceful Conflict*; Hugh Hanning, *The Peaceful Uses of Military Forces* (New York: Frederick A. Praeger in cooperation with the World Veterans Federation, 1967); and Harry F. Waterhouse, *A Time to Build* (Columbia: University of South Carolina Press, 1964).

3. This account is taken from Glick, *Peaceful Conflict*, pp. 59–66, and 186. Another version of this episode appears in Glick, "Alaskan Civic Action," *Military Review* 46 (December 1966), pp. 57–61.

The veterinary civic action was especially important for a number of reasons that Americans in the Lower Forty-Eight States are not usually aware of. First, the economic livelihood of so many of Alaska's Eskimoes and Indians depends upon the health of their dogs, which they must use for transportation. Second, there were at the time no civilian veterinarians within 500 miles of Nome or north of Fairbanks. And third, the vaccine for the animals is quite expensive for the average Indian or Eskimo.

The work went well and was appreciated by civilians. In one article in a local paper, a person wrote: "We thank them for all the help they gave to the people here and we thank those who sent them here." In another, the mayor of Nome reportedly thanked the army "personnel as well as local aides Bob Emmonds and Lawrence Kayoukluk for assisting in taking care of the canine welfare of our town." In a third, the regional sanitarian for all of Alaska north of the Alaska Range was said to have expressed "the appreciation of the State Division of Health to the army for their cooperation."

The Alaskan Indians and Eskimoes helped by army medical, dental, and veterinary personnel in 1965 are still there. They still need such help. They need it on a regular and not an ad hoc basis, as do others in the remote corners of that and every other state in the union. There are Indians, blacks, Puerto Ricans, Mexican-Americans, migrant workers, whites and others all over the country who are poor, old, or sick. Many of them can't get medical attention not only because they can't pay for it, but also because there aren't enough civilian medical personnel to go around.

In 1966, the year after Exercise Polar Strike, I went to visit a friend who was being treated in one of the largest hospitals in Philadelphia. When I got there, I took a wrong turn down a corridor and was shocked to find a whole, fully equipped wing that was shut down because of a shortage of nurses and other specialists. That was the year in which United States Public Health Service statistics showed 750,000 available full-time jobs for registered nurses, but only 621,000 R. N.s who were working. And 80,000 of them were working part-time. The USPHS predicted that the number of full-time nursing positions in 1970 would increase to 850,000, but that the number of both full- and part-time nurses would only reach 680,000.[4]

Someday, hopefully very soon, national budgets, national priorities, and national manpower utilization will be rearranged. Then, the nursing shortage and other pressing domestic problems will be solved by conventional means. But until that day, we ought to consider unconventional means. With regard to medicine, we ought to use the

---

4. *New York Times*, 1 August 1966, p. 20.

existing "Armed Forces Entrance and Examination Stations for large-scale diagnostic health examinations by civilian agencies."[5] We ought to assign both reserve and regular military medical units to some of the overburdened or nearly nonexistent civilian hospitals and clinics in the cities, small towns, Indian reservations, and rural slum and poverty areas of America. There may, in fact, be a plan to do just that. Speaking before a group of fiscal officers of the hospitals of Greater Philadelphia in the fall of 1969, Pennsylvania's Budget Secretary David O. Maxwell said that he "understood that the U. S. Department of Health, Education and Welfare already has a plan for utilizing military medical corpsmen in that role, and intends to put it into effect when hostilities in Vietnam cease."[6] Finally, we ought to at least try the suggestion of the American Academy of General Practice that doctors who work for two years in ghettos or in areas without physicians be exempted from military service.[7]

Americans today are probably more innovative, more sensitive, and more compassionate than they have ever been before. Indeed many of them say they are revolutionaries, ready to try and do new things to solve the ills of "the system." In the absence of an *existing* civilian alternative solution to one of "the system's" most vexing ills, to refuse to use *temporarily* an available military instrument for the alleviation of widespread pain and suffering is at best doctrinaire and at worst immoral. Perhaps what I am suggesting "isn't the answer. But what else is? It's about time somebody started finding out."[8]

---

5. *Army Digest* 24 (January 1969), p. 71.
6. Quoted in the *Philadelphia Bulletin*, 25 September 1969, p. 10.
7. Ibid., 30 September 1969, p. 14.
8. These are the words of Ted Watkins, director of the Watts Labor Community Action Committee. He was speaking of a plan he conceived and executed with the cooperation of the Defense Department, the Office of Economic Opportunity, and the President's Council on Youth Opportunity to send black children from the Watts section of Los Angeles to summer camp at Camp Roberts, California. For more details of this experiment, see *New York Times*, 3 September 1967, p. 36.

10

The Congress and the Complex: "Who's Deceivin' Who?"

In the early 1950s I moved to Florida, where I lived for five years. My first experience there in political relevance and reality was in watching a primary fight for the governorship in what was then a completely one-party state. Unlike the situation nowadays, a Republican then simply had no chance at all. The real contest was among about half a dozen Southern Democrats whose only major difference was that some were more segregationist and antiblack and others were less so.

The most liberal of the candidates, relatively speaking, ran up and down the Sunshine State shouting: "Who's deceivin' who, I ask ya, who's deceivin' who?" He lost. And I am still trying to figure out whether it was because of his politics, his style, his personality, or the nauseating number of times he repeated his campaign slogan.

In using this anecdote, I am not trying to suggest that Congress *as a whole* has been deceiving the American people with regard to the machinations of the military-industrial complex. Indeed, it is the other way around. It is Congress that has allowed itself to be deceived, along with the rest of the American people. However, I am suggesting that Congress must take a great deal of the blame for the real sins of the military, its contractors, and its consultants. After all, Congress pays the piper and it is supposed to investigate what it is paying for and why. Congress has the means, if not the will, to eliminate or control some of the more flagrant abuses of the military-industrial complex. It has generally failed to use them. Instead, it has preferred to deflect the nation's wrath in this regard from itself to other agencies and institutions in and out of government. To the extent that it has done this, it has let us all down.

With regard to the Vietnam tragedy, for example, Congress has been getting away with murder. It became quite fashionable in the late 1960s for more and more congressmen and senators from both parties to vie with one another in deploring the war, with its high casualties and even higher material costs. They deplored it mainly on moral, political, and economic grounds. But these same grounds for pain and protest existed in the 1950s and the early 1960s too. As Robert D. Cantor, one of my graduate students, put it in a seminar paper he wrote for me in the last days of 1969:

> We are now hopefully in the final stages of a war that has seen over 200,000 casualties and severe economic dislocation. The accompanying protest by usually nonprotesting segments of society is probably a function of inflation as much as conscience. . . . [Killing] was just as immoral in 1961 as it is today. The threat to our security from North Vietnam was no greater nor is the reason for our being in South Vietnam different today than in 1964 at the time of the Johnson–Goldwater election. Why didn't the senators who have been in full voice in condemnation of the war for the past year raise their protests when escalation might have been prevented? The reasons cannot logically be explained on moral grounds nor can they be based on strategy considerations. The only plausible explanation of the rising disenchantment is that for the first time Americans are feeling the economic strains of the war. The number of casualties is large but affects very few families; the fact is that until the inflation started to accelerate two years ago, very few people were inconvenienced in any way and income rose quickly in all sectors.

He went on to say that "there is something very wrong about a war that allows men to die while their fellow citizens at home luxuriate in increased wages and profits."

One may not agree with Cantor, especially with his contention that the country's conscience follows casualties and its pocketbook. That is a matter of individual viewpoint. But is is true that Congress delayed or avoided imposing civilian taxes and controls that a war of such magnitude, regardless of its popularity, morality, or wisdom, would seem to require. If high defense budgets and the Vietnam War are indeed the major causes of our inflation, Congress must take much of the blame because of the military appropriations it made, the non-military appropriations it should not have made, and the civilian wage, price, and other controls it did not impose or imposed much too late.

In speaking of the war in Vietnam earlier, I said I did not think that Congress "made military appropriations it did not want to make" and that "our military involvement there could have ended whenever Congress had the will and the courage to stop supplying money for it." A lot of congressmen attacked the war in 1968, 1969, and 1970. But where were they in 1965, 1966, and 1967? Why did the nation have to wait until 1969 for someone such as Senator Charles E. Goodell of New York to introduce his "Vietnam Disengagement Act," one of whose clauses states quite specifically that "no part of any amount authorized to be appropriated under any Act shall be used after 1 December 1970, to maintain military personnel of the United States in Vietnam?" Whether the Goodell Bill was wise or stupid is not really the point: what is important is that it joined the issues of morality, money, and militarism and gave his legislative colleagues a chance to put their votes where their voices and presumably their convictions are.

There are other senators besides Goodell who say they oppose the Vietnam War and the military-industrial complex. Among the more prominent are J. William Fulbright of Arkansas, Philip A. Hart of Michigan, George S. McGovern of South Dakota, Eugene J. McCarthy of Minnesota, Gaylord Nelson and William Proxmire of Wisconsin, and Edward M. Kennedy of Massachusetts. Many of them joined a group of 9 senators and 36 congressmen on 1 June 1969 in issuing a warning against our becoming a "national security state." They said: "The most urgent challenge confronting Congress today is to reassert control over the military bureaucracy and the policy decisions it has preempted."[1]

Somewhat earlier, in a speech he delivered at Yeshiva University in December 1968, Senator McGovern called the military-industrial complex "the most serious internal threat facing the United States on the eve of the Nixon Administration." He said that "a central question facing the new Administration and the American people will be whether we use the $30 billion now being squandered in Vietnam to improve the quality of our society or permit it to be gobbled up by the military for a new string of gadgets and adventures such as the ill-advised antiballistic missile system."[2]

Nevertheless, what did Senator McGovern and other legislators do when they were given a roll-call opportunity to synchronize their

---

1. Quoted in *New York Times*, 2 June 1969, p. 10.
2. Ibid., 10 December 1968, p. 24.

voices, their views, and their votes? On 20 March 1967, H.R. 7123, a bill appropriating more than $12 billion in supplemental funds for Vietnam, came up for final passage on the floor of the Senate. It passed by 77 to 3, the 3 being Senators Gaylord Nelson, Wayne Morse of Oregon, and Ernest Gruening of Alaska. (Morse and Gruening were both defeated in the elections of 1968.) Fulbright voted for it, Proxmire voted for it, Kennedy voted for it, even McCarthy and McGovern voted for it, as they did for S-666, a bill which authorized appropriations of over $20 billion for defense research and development and for procurement of airplanes, naval vessels, tracked combat vehicles, and missiles.[3] The same thing happened in the House of Representatives. The Vietnam Supplemental bill, H.R. 7123, passed there on 16 March 1967 by a vote of 385 to 11. Goodell of New York, then a congressman, voted for it, as did half of the 36 congressmen then in office who signed the 1969 statement warning Americans against a national security state.[4]

If our national legislators, some of whom aspire to the presidency, speak one way about Vietnam and unbridled militarism but vote another way, it becomes proper to wonder whether the congressional credibility gap is as wide as, if not wider than, whatever other gaps there are in our national body politic.

It would be shortsighted to tie the sins that Congress shares with the military-industrial complex only to the Vietnam War and its aftermath. Our Vietnam fixation has clouded our collective vision and interfered with objective scrutiny of all kinds of non-Vietnam issues. Congress has aided, abetted, or simply overlooked the abuses of the military-industrial complex for decades before Vietnam. And it will continue to do so if the public, because of inertia, fatigue, elation at the winding-down or end of the war, or what-have-you, allows it.

What are some of the most serious complaints against the military-industrial complex made by people who are *not* pacifists, who are *not* for the immediate doing away of our armed forces and its suppliers, who have *not* lost faith in the American Dream, and who do *not* want to destroy The System? And what can and should Congress do about them?

If one made a short list of some of the worst features of the military-industrial complex, especially as they relate to congressional actions and inactions, it might look something like this:

1. Too many defense installations.
2. Too much mismanagement and profiteering.
3. Too many retired officers in defense industry.

---

3. *The Congressional Quarterly Almanac* 23 (1967), p. 14–S.
4. Ibid., pp. 14–H, 15–H.

4. Too many pro-military congressmen.
5. Too much nonmilitary research by the military.
6. Too few congressmen who can understand the technical and economic complexities of defense requests.
7. Too much "public relations" by the military and their allies.

Let's examine the items on this list in some detail.

TOO MANY DEFENSE INSTALLATIONS

Every budget has its fat, every organization its dead wood. This is as true for the Defense Department as it is for any other private or public agency of any size. Yet what happens in the Congress of the United States of America any time the Pentagon announces its intention to cut, combine, or close military installations in this country?

Congressmen and senators, Republicans and Democrats, Northerners and Southerners, Easterners and Westerners, liberals and conservatives, Vietnam hawks and Vietnam doves, those who are pro-Pentagon and those who are anti-Pentagon, fiscal spendthrifts and fiscal tightwads all rise up and fight to defend their "territory" from the encroachments of the "enemy." Our legislators, when they behave this way, seem to be giving additional proof of the point that Robert Ardrey tries to make in his book, *The Territorial Imperative: A Personal Inquiry into the Animal Origins of Property and Nations*.[5]

Consider: In the spring of 1969 Secretary of Defense Melvin R. Laird, himself a former member of the House of Representatives, announced that he was going to eliminate 687 of the 1,026 jobs at the Naval Applied Science Laboratory, located in the former Brooklyn Navy Yard. He said that this was part of a national effort intended to trim the military budget by $95 million dollars a year, do away nationally with more than 3,000 civilian jobs, transfer more than 6,000 uniformed men to other tasks, and make more than 14,000 acres of Pentagon-owned property available for civilian uses.

New York City and New York State are not nearly as dependent upon defense employment as, for example, Southern California. Regardless, the head of CLICK, the Commerce Labor Industry Corporation of Kings County (Brooklyn), immediately told the navy that this would "strike another serious blow to our already depressed area." Congressman Emanuel Celler of Brooklyn announced that the New York State congressional delegation was inviting the navy secretary to "discuss the purported justification for this action." He added: "While we certainly would endorse actions designed to effect savings and increase efficiency," we want "to make sure that these would

---

5. Ardrey, *The Territorial Imperative* (New York: Atheneum, 1966).

in fact be brought about by the proposed restructuring and more than compensate for the disruption to personnel involved and their families."[6]

The same predictable reaction occurred in the fall of 1969. This time Secretary Laird made an announcement calling for the eventual elimination of over 64,000 military and civilian jobs and the consolidation, reduction, realignment, or closing of 307 bases and operations all over the country and abroad. The intention was to save $609 million a year. This time it was not Democratic Congressman Celler, but the two liberal Republican Senators Charles E. Goodell and Jacob K. Javits who took up the cudgels on behalf of New York. They issued a statement saying they were going to investigate whether New York was suffering a "disproportionate share" of base closings both in the past and in the present.[7]

The reaction of Pennsylvania, where I live and work, to the proposed transfer of certain research and development functions away from the Frankford Arsenal in Philadelphia is another case in point. All through the spring, summer, and fall of 1969, city officials, business groups, and the entire Pennsylvania delegation in both Houses of Congress fought a running battle with the Department of Defense over the Arsenal, winning a temporary respite from the "enemy" in Washington. The battle leader was Hugh Scott, now Minority Leader of the Senate, who was up for reelection in 1970. When asked in September 1969 whether the army would eventually cancel its plans for the Frankford Arsenal altogether, he frankly admitted that he didn't really know. But he said that if it didn't, "there will be a lot of blood on the floor."[8]

Earlier, in a 30 June 1969 statewide newsletter, he used the word "confrontation" and described the planned cutback at the Arsenal as a move "against the national interest." He also reprinted a cartoon by the *Philadelphia Bulletin*'s cartoonist Borsstedt, which shows Scott standing atop the walls of a beleaguered fort, next to a tattered flag marked "Frankford Arsenal." He and the others in the fort, including Pennsylvania's other Republican Senator, Richard S. Schweiker, are wearing what appear to be Civil War uniforms. Schweiker is passing cannon balls marked "Political Clout" up to Scott, who is ramming them into an artillery piece with the shout: "Take aim on the Pentagon, men!"

Economically speaking, the reaction of Pennsylvanians to defense cuts in their own backyard was entirely typical. It was in keeping with the decades-long trend of both Congress and its constituents to let local economic considerations overwhelm any other considerations

---

6. Quoted in *New York Times*, 20 May 1969, p. 93.
7. Ibid., 28 October 1969, p. 1.
8. Quoted in *Philadelphia Bulletin*, 7 September 1969, p. 16.

in defense budget decisions. And the *Philadelphia Bulletin*'s editorial writer was behaving no differently from those of many other newspapers across the land when he wrote:

> Overlooked entirely by the Defense Department was the harsh effect the proposed movement, and the closing of the entire Arsenal, would have on the city's economy. The Arsenal has [over 5,300 employees and] a $57 million annual payroll. Taking this away from the area would have the net effect of a loss of $384 million in direct and indirect benefits.
>
> Rather than move the Arsenal, the mayor's task force asks that it become the site for the entire proposed Weapons Research and Development Center.[9]

However, Philadelphia's Frankford Arsenal story had a curious, less typical side to it, too. It is one that, if repeated elsewhere with great intensity, may prove much more intractable to deal with than mere economic concerns. It was the side that had to do with race relations.

If it is a contradiction to oppose high defense budgets and the Vietnam War because they badly skew our national priorities and yet oppose defense cutbacks because they hurt our local economies, is it not more a contradiction to be against such cutbacks because they represent "racism" and "unconscionable" discrimination against blacks? This is exactly what was charged when the Frankford Arsenal story "broke" in Philadelphia in 1969.

Upon hearing of it, Charles W. Bowser, executive director of the Philadelphia Urban Coalition, wrote to Secretary of Defense Laird that the proposed changes at the Arsenal would eliminate 787 jobs held by blacks and would transfer away from the city another 164 jobs being filled by black employees. He further told the secretary:

> In addition to the compelling reasons for maintaining the arsenal in this city, I specifically and vehemently protest this apparent elimination of every black employee from this federal facility.
>
> At a time when the nation should be deeply concerned with repairing the racial fabric of our society which has been torn by injustice and oppression, it is inconceivable that the Defense Department would be responsible for the wholesale firing of 787 black people and the elimination in this city of all positions held by blacks at Frankford Arsenal.

Saying that he could not accept the consequences of the government's decision "as mere coincidence or accident," Bowser continued:

---

9. Ibid., 13 September 1969, p. 6.

Black Americans who still believe in their native land and are still willing to work for its improvement rather than encourage its destruction are seriously undermined and publicly repudiated by federal decisions which are more consistent with racism than with justice.

This city and every other American city exists from day to day on the brink of that foreboding social chasm which is splitting our society. Many men of all colors and persuasions are working to bridge the cleft and weld a harmonious community. Their efforts are all but destroyed by repeated attacks on small symbols of progress.

Whatever the reason for the initial decision, the consequences of that decision are unconscionable and it must be reversed. I await your reply.[10]

Under such circumstances, what are Pentagon budget-cutters and liberal congressmen to do!

TOO MUCH MISMANAGEMENT AND PROFITEERING

More and more, America's comprehensive newspapers are publishing stories and editorials with headlines such as:

AUDITING MILITARY CONTRACTS

OFFICIALS ACCUSED OF LAXITY IN U.S. CONTRACT OVER-PRICING

CONTRACT LOSSES TOTAL $8.8 BILLION

MANY EXPLOIT FREE GOVERNMENT EQUIPMENT

DEFENSE PROFITS CALLED TOO HIGH

TO DISARM A TIGER: CAN THE MILITARY-INDUSTRIAL COMPLEX BE TAMED WITHOUT NATIONALIZING IT?

THE NEW "WAR PROFITEERS"[11]

The last article was written by James Reston of the *New York Times* in 1968, the year in which more than half of the $80 billion dollar defense budget (or 25 percent of the then total federal budget) went for procurement.[12] In his article Reston wrote: "Every war has produced a new crop of 'war profiteers,' and the Vietnam war is no exception. What is original now is that the arts of cheating the government are improving and the techniques for exposing the profiteers are declining."

10. Quoted in ibid., 24 May 1969, pp. 1, 3.

11. The first two headlines are from ibid., 12 August 1969, p. 20; and 1 December 1969, p. 43. The others are from the *New York Times*, 29 November 1968, p. 9; 29 November 1967, p. 35; 18 June 1968, p. 3; 19 November 1969, p. 77; and 3 May 1968, p. 46.

12. U.S., Congress, Joint Economic Committee, *The Economics of Military Procurement: Report of the Subcommittee on Economy in Government.* 91st Cong., 1st Sess. (Washington, D.C.: Government Printing Office, May 1969), p. 1.

Reston is right, of course. But, after all, the kind of thing he is describing—whether one calls it cheating or by some other name—has been going on for many years, even when we were not involved in a Vietnam or any other war. No government can be cheated unless it lets itself be, just as no lady in search of love can be seduced unless she wants to be. And if the techniques of defense against war profiteering (or seduction) are indeed declining, this is because the government (like the young lady) isn't really keen about shoring them up.

Reston focuses his attention on the Renegotiation Board, which Congress established in 1951. The Board is responsible for eliminating any excess profits that may have flowed through the sieve to defense contractors and subcontractors. The sieve, composed of such elements as the Defense Department itself, the Renegotiation Board, Congress' own General Accounting Office, and the president's Bureau of the Budget, is very leaky. It is very leaky because Congress, until now at least, has allowed it to be. And it makes no difference, in the final analysis, whether Congress has failed in this watchdog function because of action, inaction, indifference, ignorance, or connivance.

According to Reston, in 1952 the Renegotiation Board had more than 500 employees. Presumably they were mostly accountants, auditors, and other kinds of economic investigators. During the Korean War alone, they were able to get back more than $800 million through the renegotiated contracts they forced upon defense suppliers. Nevertheless, in 1968, with a vastly increased military procurement budget and a war as bloody as anything in Korea, the Board's personnel roster was allowed to fall to about 180.

Congress has also whittled away at the Board's authority. Originally, all contracts of $250,000 and above came under the Board's review. Then, in 1954, Congress exempted all defense contracts under $500,000. In 1956 it did the same thing for those under $1,000,000. Additionally, Congress took away the Board's right to supervise certain categories of goods, such as machinery and tools with a useful life of more than five years, and also certain so-called standard commercial articles or services.

The Renegotiation Board is only one part of the scenario of mismanagement, nonmanagement, and profiteering that Congress has helped the military-industrial complex write. One of the other "scenes" is the steady decrease of formally advertised and competitive contracts and the steady increase of noncompetitive, so-called single source awards. About 90 percent of defense procurement contracts are awarded single source. This situation is so bad that Senator William Proxmire's Subcommittee on Economy in Government reported in May 1969 "a record low for competition and a record high for single source procurement over the past five years."[13]

A third scene is higher and higher prices and profit pyramiding between contractors and subcontractors. A fourth is cost overruns and voluminous "change orders" in already awarded contracts. Still others are "loose handling of government-owned property, interest-free financing of contractors, absence of comprehensive profits reports and studies, lack of uniform accounting standards, reverse [performance and delivery] incentives, and a special patent policy lucrative to the contractor."[14]

The government's patent policy toward defense contractors is particularly obnoxious for it "tends to reduce competition and increase the concentration of economic power." As the Proxmire Committee pointed out, it permits a contractor:

> to obtain exclusive patent rights, free of charge, on inventions produced in the performance of government contracts. The Defense Department normally retains a nonexclusive royalty-free license for itself. The contractor, in other words, obtains a monopoly which he can exploit for his own private gain in the commercial market for inventions paid for by public moneys. This "fringe benefit" of doing business under government contracts does not get reported as part of the contractor's profits. In effect, the public pays twice. Once through the government contract; again in the marketing of the private monopoly.
>
> It should be noted that the contractor's own patent policy differs from that of the Department of Defense. When contractors award contracts to independent research institutes, the contractors, not the research institutes, retain the patent rights. Further, the employees of contractors generally must agree that the contractor gets the patent rights to any inventions developed during their employment.
>
> [Moreover, . . .] permitting contractors to obtain patent rights from government contracts reduces competition in defense industries because the "ins" get a competitive advantage over the "outs." . . .
>
> In contrast to general government policy, the Atomic Energy Commission and the National Aeronautics and Space Administration are required by law to take government title to inventions developed under government contracts, subject to waiver of rights by the government. The government's [present] policy [except for the AEC and NASA] amounts to a special privilege to contractors at the expense of the taxpayers.[15]

What can Congress do about some of these abuses? First of all, it has to *want* to do something about them. Second, it can rid itself

---

13. Ibid., p. 4.
14. Ibid.
15. Ibid., p. 7.

of the notion that we must buy defense, in the words of former Defense Secretary Robert S. McNamara, "the way women buy perfume." Congressmen, like women, he says, believe that "if it costs more, . . . it must be better."[16] Third, Congress can change its giveaway patent policy. Fourth, it can look seriously into the suggestion of the late Walter F. Reuther of the United Auto Workers Union that 25 percent of a defense contractor's profits after taxes be put into a peace fund to finance conversion to consumer-oriented production.[17] Fifth, it can give the Renegotiation Board the money, men, and authority it needs to do some real renegotiating. It can do the same thing for the General Accounting Office, so that GAO can do the kind of pre- and post-audits we really need to monitor defense contract spending.

It is not to Congress' credit that it has, at this writing, still not seen fit to pass a proposal of Pennsylvania's Senator Richard S. Schweiker. Schweiker would subject defense contracts to strict quarterly audits by the GAO and give GAO the power to subpoena the records of any diffident contractors.[18] Until Congress passes the Schweiker proposal, or something similar, one has the right to question whether it really wants to cut defense spending and defense contractors' abuses. As the *Philadelphia Bulletin* (the same paper that fought so valiantly to save the Frankford Arsenal for Philadelphia) editorialized:

> The American military establishment is not solely to blame if defense costs have gotten out of hand. Minimizing what projects will cost is a game that is widely played throughout government, with congressmen often willing participants.
>
> If congressmen required more information to exercise their responsibility on military costs and if expanded auditing by GAO was desirable, Congress could have acted to get the information and impose added controls years ago.[19]

TOO MANY RETIRED OFFICERS IN DEFENSE INDUSTRY

In March 1969 Senator William Proxmire issued a report showing that the number of colonels, navy captains, generals, and admirals who went to work in defense industries after their retirement had tripled since 1959. Only 721 such retirees were working in defense industries in 1959; ten years later the number was 2,072. Said the senator: "This is a most dangerous and shocking condition. It indicates the increasing influence of the big contractors with the military and the military with the big contractors."[20]

---

16. Quoted in *Philadelphia Bulletin*, 24 June 1969, p. 43.
17. For details, see *New York Times*, 2 December 1969, p. 22.
18. *Philadelphia Bulletin*, 6 November 1969, p. 38.
19. Ibid., 12 August 1969, p. 20.
20. Quoted in *New York Times*, 23 March 1969, p. 32.

Here again, we have another of those situations involving the military-industrial complex which most congressmen either encourage, ignore, or remain content merely to complain about verbally. If Congress can restrict the amount of extra income that retired civilians can earn without losing part or all of their pension dollars under Social Security, why can't it restrict or stop entirely the movement of retired, pensioned officers into defense industry? Given cost overruns and other evidences of economic license, it might actually save the country millions of dollars if we retired career military officers after 20 or 30 years of service at 100 percent or more of their highest base pay, with the strictly enforced stipulation that they may never work for any company for pay, especially defense companies.

Such a plan may or may not be economically and constitutionally feasible. Congress ought to try and find out. If it is not feasible, then some other one is. More appalling than the large number of high-ranking military retirees working for the defense contractors is Congress' steadfast refusal to do anything effective about it.

TOO MANY PRO-MILITARY CONGRESSMEN

The tendency for members of Congress, especially the chairmen of committees and subcommittees dealing with the military, to favor their clientele is well-known. The late Drew Pearson built a considerable portion of his journalistic fame shooting at congressmen such as South Carolina's L. Mendel Rivers, head of the House Armed Services Committee. Pearson was especially incensed at what he considered to be the you-scratch-my-back-and-I'll-scratch-yours relationship between certain congressmen and the military.[21]

I have already shown how Congressman F. Edward Hébert and his colleagues on the Special Subcommittee on Service Academies were, in almost a thousand pages of printed testimony, unable to see any shortcomings in these military educational institutions. There are serious shortcomings at West Point, Annapolis, and Colorado Springs. These places are not the only sources of military wisdom and leadership. One of our greatest generals was George C. Marshall, who was graduated from the Virginia Military Institute and not the United States Military Academy. Yet one would hardly guess this from the attitude of Congress, which is not yet ready to mandate that an increasingly higher number of our generals and admirals should come from the ranks of qualified colonels and navy captains who are not academy graduates.

Another questionable interaction between national legislators and the armed forces is the high number of senators and congressmen

---

21. See, for example, his column "Rivers Blocks Probes of Military Fiascos," *Philadelphia Bulletin*, 28 May 1969, p. 56.

who find it so necessary to be in the military reserves. In 1964 they numbered 74; in 1969, 139. A hundred were from the House of Representatives and 39 from the Senate.[22] How many legislatures of other democracies allow 40 percent of the members of their upper chamber and more than 25 percent of those in their lower chamber to serve in the military reserves?

Senator Strom Thurmond of South Carolina and Congressman Robert L. F. Sikes of Florida are major generals in the Army Reserve. Senators Howard W. Cannon of Nevada and Barry Goldwater of Arizona are major generals in the Air Force Reserve. Congressman William S. Maillaird of California is a rear admiral in the Naval Reserve. The four senators are on the Senate Armed Services Committee. Congressman Maillaird is a ranking member of the House committee dealing with the Merchant Marine. Congressman Sikes is chairman of the Military Construction Appropriations Subcommittee and number two man in the House Defense Appropriations Subcommittee.

Everyone can interpret these facts as he wishes. Some will interpret them as additional examples of conflict of interest; others, as additional illustrations of militarism. To avoid such negative interpretations altogether, Congress should say to its collective self: "Each of us can be members of the national legislature or we can be in the military reserves, but we cannot be in both at the same time. We must choose. If we want to be senators or congressmen, we cannot be generals or admirals. If we want to be generals or admirals, we cannot be senators or congressmen." At the very least, Congress ought not to allow any of its members who are high-ranking officers in the reserves to sit on any of its committees dealing with the armed services.

TOO MUCH NONMILITARY RESEARCH BY THE MILITARY

Some years ago, Congress passed an important law providing federal funds for the improvement of high school and college teaching of foreign languages, foreign areas studies, science, mathematics, and so on. It felt compelled to call that law "The National Defense Education Act," and not "The National Education Act." Why did it do this? Why did it insert the word "defense"—with all of its connotations—into a law that would be justifiable and acceptable in the most peaceful of times and the most disarmed of countries? Was Congress reflecting the American mood, or was it helping to mold it?

I said earlier that the distinction between military and nonmilitary research is often a matter of definition and budget location. I said also that if the Department of Defense had in some respects become

22. Pilisuk, "A Reply to Roger Little," *American Journal of Orthopsychiatry* 38, p. 880; and *Philadelphia Inquirer*, 4 May 1969, p. 1.

our version of the Soviet Academy of Sciences, it was because Congress had allowed it to become so. It is Congress that has given the Defense Department very high research budgets and most other agencies in and out of government much lower ones. It is Congress that has allowed the Pentagon to fund with these budgets research projects that seem to many to lie more logically elsewhere. If the Pentagon is now beginning to move away from supporting projects not directly related to its military mission, it is only because Congress has finally begun to force it to.

Congress banned military sponsorship of nonmilitary research in section 203 of the Military Procurement Authorization Act for fiscal year 1970 (Public Law 91–121): "None of the funds authorized to be appropriated by this Act may be used to carry out any research project or study unless such project or study has a direct or apparent relationship to a specific military function or operation."[23] What Congress did in 1969, it can do regularly in future years. It can go further. It can transfer *all* basic research funds to the National Science Foundation and the National Institutes of Health. It can transfer *all* foreign areas research funds to agencies such as the State Department. But will it?

TOO FEW CONGRESSMEN WHO UNDERSTAND THE TECHNICAL AND ECONOMIC COMPLEXITIES OF DEFENSE REQUESTS

Very few, if any, members of Congress are scientists, engineers, economists, or professional specialists in military strategy, tactics, equipment, and costs. Most of them are lawyers and businessmen. Lawyers and businessmen can have good intuition and insight into these matters, and Congress does have the Legislative Reference Service of the Library of Congress and the expertise of congressional committee staffs and consultants. Usually, however, none of these are a real match for the arsenal of defense facts, figures, and factotums that the Executive Branch of government can muster against Congress.

This has always been a problem for the thoughtful congressman. It is worse now because very complex and costly technologies and manpower utilizations are so much a part of the problem of avoiding or engaging in military confrontations. To resolve this problem, Dr. Ralph E. Lapp, who helped to develop the first atomic bomb and who

---

23. See U.S., Congress, House of Representatives, *Mission Agency Support of Basic Research: Report to the Subcommittee on Science, Research, and Development of the Committee on Science and Astronautics*, Serial L, 91st Cong., 2nd Sess. (Washington, D.C.: Government Printing Office, 1970): note the recommendation calling for "support for those high-quality research projects dropped by the [Defense] Department by reason of section 203 which should be continued in the national interest" (p. 5).

is now a frequent critic of what he calls "defense socialism," has suggested the creation of a National Analysis Council. It would provide Congress with "authoritative independent advice on techno-military problems."[24] One of my students, Floyd E. Stoner, has suggested some ways in which such a council might work. According to Stoner, Congress would establish a permanent joint committee of both Houses to oversee the council. To prevent political patronage and the domination of powerful senators and congressmen with a particular viewpoint, the committee's membership would be changed frequently and the committee would not be subject to the usual rules of seniority.

As for the analysts and consultants on the council, they would come from among the nation's most distinguished nongovernmental specialists in foreign and defense policy, budgeting and cost analysis, defense economics, military procurement and technology, and related fields. To prevent the council from becoming a self-perpetuating congressional "think tank" with its own self-serving interests, each of its members would be given one-time, nonrenewable contracts of, let us say, two years at salaries that could not be matched elsewhere. They would be chosen randomly from the longest possible list of the best available people. Each of them would advise Congress during its investigations, debates, and decisions. Whenever desirable and possible, each advisor would do his own independent research, analyze his own data, and reach his own conclusions before presenting them to Congress.

Whether such a plan will work in actual practice, only experience and time will tell. But if it doesn't, something similar is badly needed. Otherwise, Congress will never even approach a position of informational and technical equality with those in the defense establishment who come before it for authorizations and allocations.

TOO MUCH PUBLIC RELATIONS BY THE MILITARY

What can be said anew about this problem has already been said very well by Senator J. William Fulbright. Reacting to a navy public relations program that he said included the making of films and the organizing of cruises to Hawaii for businessmen, newspaper editors, and reporters, he remarked in December 1969:

I am reminded of W.C. Fields's admonition, "Never give a sucker an even break."
With the three services and the Department of Defense and their allies in industry, academia and labor all working at convincing the taxpayer

---

24. Ralph E. Lapp, "The Weapons Industry is a Menace," *Saturday Evening Post* (15 June 1968), pp. 10, 16.

that he must shell out more for military purposes, John Q. Public doesn't stand a chance—unless his representatives in the Congress bring the public relations apparatus under control. [25]

Congress has been to the military-industrial complex what the universal joint is to a car. Without the joint, the car can't operate. Without Congress, neither can the complex. Over the past three decades, the American Congress has been the major governmental contributor to the erosion of the constitutional principle of civilian control of the military. But now, "for the first time, along with the growing realization that Vietnam has proved a disaster, Congress is moving, with something more than its traditional lead-footed pace, toward the realization that if it doesn't balance domestic against military priorities, no one else seems very likely to." [26]

25. Quoted in *New York Times*, 3 December 1969, p. 22.
26. Warren Weaver, Jr., ibid., 10 August 1969, p. E—2.

11

A Summing Up

Any reader who has come along with me this far realizes that my main aim has been to get some new ideas into the system. For example: a draft lottery that would be extended to women and to nonmilitary service, professors consulting to the military for free, the possible retirement of military officers at 100 percent pay in return for *iron-clad* prohibitions against their working for the Defense Department or its contractors, the merging or elimination of our existing military academies, congressional mandating of a higher portion of promotions to general and flag officer ranks from among nonacademy graduates, and the end of the congressman-reservist.

In addition, any reader who has come along with me this far also knows of my belief that, unfortunately, military realities outside of the United States still require some American warriors, weapons, and weapons-makers, and the money to pay for them. Hopefully, all of this will be at diminished levels and more for readiness than for use. He may have guessed that I am terribly worried that America's foreign policy pendulum is swinging from the one extreme of World Policeman to the other of Global Dropout. We have, in fact, already moved from an era of too many old and ill-conceived military commitments to perhaps an era of no new ones, regardless of the merits of the cases involved. In the end, this new extreme, if it persists, may prove as costly and as dangerous as the old one.

I have, of course, shown how unexpected, even unintended, benefits can and do flow from the military-industrial complex. But I do not want to be misunderstood. I do not want that complex to exist a moment longer than is necessary. I do not want it to do any nonmilitary things that other segments of our society and government can and *will* do faster and better, even if not more cheaply. And I certainly do not want it to be uncontrolled and uncriticized. But there is a world of difference between restraining and redirecting the military-industrial complex, and hobbling, humiliating, and prematurely destroying it altogether. To do the latter in today's unsettling world would be disastrous. Not do to the former in today's unsettling America would be unconscionable.

Bibliography

PRIMARY SOURCES

Unpublished Materials

Documents

U.S. Army. "Army Reserve Officers' Training Corps Fact Sheet" (1 April 1969). Supplied by the Department of Military Science of Temple University.

U.S. "Commissioned Officer Retention." Attachment to a letter from Major General E. H. Burba, Deputy Commanding General of the First United States Army, 10 December 1968.

U.S. "Survey of Off-Base Housing." Attachment to a letter from Brigadier General William E. Ekman, Coordinator for Off-Base Housing Services, Department of Defense, 10 October 1967.

U.S. Department of Defense. "They Speak for Themselves: Statements [on Housing Discrimination] by Military Personnel in the Metropolitan Washington Area." Section V of an untitled document supplied by the Defense Department, n.d.

Webster College. St. Louis, Missouri. "VAULT—Veterans Accelerated Urban Learning for Teaching." Attachment to a letter from Donald W. White, Director of VAULT, 21 October 1969.

Letters to the Author

Barton, Colonel William G., Directorate of Personnel Training and Education, Office of the Air Force Deputy Chief of Staff for Personnel, 13 March 1968.

Bennett, L. Howard, Director for Civil Rights, Department of Defense, 12 December 1968 and 26 March 1969.

De Camp, Captain D. E., Director, Management Information Support Division, Bureau of Naval Personnel, 25 March 1968.

Greenberg, I. M., Director, Project One Hundred Thousand, Department of Defense, 22 December 1967, 12 November 1968, and 19 May 1969.

Hays, Colonel Samuel H., Formerly with the Office of Military Psychology and Leadership, Department of Tactics, United States Military Academy, 18 November 1969.

Johnston, Chief Journalist Thomas A., Public Affairs Chief, Pacific Seabees, Commander Naval Construction Battalions, U. S. Pacific Fleet, 12 June 1969.

Ladd, Lieutenant Colonel Harvey M., Magazine and Book Branch, Directorate for Defense Information, Office of the Assistant Secretary of Defense for Public Affairs, 24 November 1969.

McKernan, Frank M., Director, Project Transition, Department of Defense, 13 November 1967.

Timpane, Phillip M., Assistant for Special Projects, Office of the Deputy Assistant Secretary of Defense for Civil Rights, 28 September 1967.

Whiting, Basil J., Program Officer, Division of National Affairs (Social Development), The Ford Foundation, 2 January 1969.

Persons Interviewed

Ball, Colonel Frank E., Assistant Director, Project One Hundred Thousand, Department of Defense, 7 December 1967.

Bennett, L. Howard, Director for Civil Rights, Department of Defense, 15 May 1969.

Greenberg, I. M., Director, Project One Hundred Thousand, Department of Defense, 15 May 1969.

Ziv, Lieutenant Colonel Yitzchak, Commandant, Israel Army's Marcus School, Haifa, 14 August 1968.

Speeches

Fulbright, J. William. "The War and its Effects—II." Speech delivered to the United States Senate, 13 December 1967.

Greenberg, I. M., "Project One Hundred Thousand: Purposes, Progress and Experience." Address before the National Security Industrial Association, Washington, D.C., 6 December 1967.

Johnson, Lyndon B. "Our Pride and Our Strength: America's Servicemen and Veterans." Message to Congress, 30 January 1968.

McNamara, Robert S. Address before the National Association of Educational Broadcasters 43rd Convention, Denver, Colorado, 7 November 1967.

Published Records and Documents

Johnston, Chief Journalist Thomas A. *"Helping Others Help Themselves."*

COMCBPAC Reports. Seabee Teams. October 1959–July 1968. Special Edition. Pearl Harbor, Hawaii: Navy Publications and Printing Service Office, 1969.

U.S. Army. *Equal Opportunity and Treatment of Military Personnel*. Regulation No. 600–6. Fort Meade, Maryland: First Army Headquarters, 14 November 1966.

U.S. Army. *Fifth Annual ROTC/NDCC Conference, 5 to 8 September 1967*. Fort Monroe, Virginia: Continental Army Command Headquarters, 1967.

U.S. Army. *Personnel Separations: Civilian Police Recruiting Program*. Circular No. 635–3. Washington, D.C.: 17 April 1968.

U.S. Army. *Reserve Components: Relief of Officers and Warrant Officers from Active Duty*. Army Regulation No. 135–173. Washington, D.C.: 31 March 1961.

U.S. Army and Air Force. *Annual Report: Chief, National Guard Bureau: Fiscal Year 1968*. Washington, D.C.: 1968.

U.S. Civil Service Commission, Bureau of Policies and Standards. *Retired Military Personnel in Federal Jobs*. Personnel Management Series No. 21. Washington, D.C.: Government Printing Office, 1969.

U.S. Congress. House of Representatives, Committee on Armed Services. *Administration of the Service Academies: Report and Hearings of the Special Subcommittee on Service Academies*, No. 66. 90th Cong., 1st and 2nd Sess. Washington, D.C.: Government Printing Office, 1968.

U.S. Congress. House of Representatives, Committee on Foreign Affairs. *Behavioral Sciences and the National Security*. House Report No. 1224. 89th Cong., 2nd Sess. Washington, D.C.: Government Printing Office, 1966.

U.S. Congress. House of Representatives, Committee on Science and Astronautics. *Centralization of Federal Science Activities: Report to the Subcommittee on Science, Research, and Development*. Serial B. 91st Cong., 1st Sess. Washington, D.C.: Government Printing Office, 1969.

U.S. Congress. House of Representatives, Committee on Science and Astronautics. *Government and Science: Hearings Before the Subcommittee on Science, Research, and Development*. No. 8. 88th Cong., 1st Sess. Washington D.C.: Government Printing Office, 1964.

U.S. Congress. House of Representatives, Committee on Science and Astronautics. *Mission Agency Support of Basic Research: Report to the Subcommittee on Science, Research, and Development*. Serial L. 91st Cong., 2nd Sess. Washington, D.C.: Government Printing Office, 1970.

U.S. Congress. House of Representatives, Committee on Science and Astronautics. *Technical Information for Congress: Report to the Subcommittee on Science, Research, and Development*. Serial A. 91st Cong., 1st Sess. Washington, D.C.: Government Printing Office, 1969.

U.S. Congress. House of Representatives, Committee on Science and Astronautics. *Technical Information for Congress: Report to the Subcommittee on Science, Research, and Development*. Serial U. 90th Cong., 2nd

Sess. Washington, D.C.: Government Printing Office, 1968.

U.S. Congress. Joint Economic Committee. *The Economics of Military Procurement: Report of the Subcommittee on Economy in Government.* 91st Cong., 1st Sess. Washington, D.C.: Government Printing Office, May 1969.

U.S. Department of Defense. *Department of Defense Conference with Governmental Affairs Committee, National Newspaper Publishers Association, 21 to 22 September 1967: Resource and Reference Book.* Washington, D.C.: 1967.

U.S. Department of Defense. *Medically Remedial Enlistment Program.* Directive No. 1304.11. Washington, D.C.: 5 December 1966, 25 April 1967.

U.S. Department of Defense. *Statement by Secretary of Defense Robert S. McNamara on the Fiscal Year 1969 to 1973 Defense Program and the 1969 Defense Budget.* Washington, D.C.: 22 January 1968.

U.S. Department of Defense. Armed Forces Information Service. *The Military Tenant.* DOD FS–46. Washington, D.C.: Government Printing Office, 1967.

U.S. Department of Defense. Office of the Assistant Secretary of Defense for Manpower and Reserve Affairs. *Project One Hundred Thousand: Characteristics and Performance of "New Standards" Men.* Washington, D.C.: September 1968.

U.S. Department of Defense. Office of the Assistant Secretary of Defense for Manpower and Reserve Affairs. *Project One Hundred Thousand: Characteristics and Performance of "New Standards" Men.* Washington, D.C.: March 1969.

U.S. Department of Defense. Office of the Assistant Secretary of Defense for Manpower and Reserve Affairs. *Report of the Special Committee on ROTC to the Secretary of Defense.* Washington, D.C.: September 1969.

U.S. Department of Defense. Office of the Assistant Secretary of Defense for Manpower. *Summary Statistics on Project One Hundred Thousand.* Washington, D.C.: October 1967.

U.S. Department of Defense. Office of the Assistant Secretary of Defense for Manpower and Reserve Affairs. *The Transition Program.* Washington, D.C.: January 1969.

U.S. Department of Defense. Office of the Director of Defense Research and Engineering. *Project Themis.* Washington, D.C.: November 1968.

U.S. Joint Chiefs of Staff. *Dictionary of United States Military Terms for Joint Usage.* JCS Pub. 1. Washington, D.C.: Government Printing Office, 1964.

U.S. National Advisory Commission on Civil Disorders. *Report.* New York: Bantam Books, 1968.

SECONDARY SOURCES
General Works and Special Studies

Ardrey, Robert. *The Territorial Imperative.* New York: Atheneum, 1966.

Bartlett, John. *Familiar Quotations.* Edited by Emily Morrison Beck. 14th ed. Boston: Little, Brown and Co., 1968.

Bridgewater, William and Kurtz, Seymour, eds. *The Columbia Encyclopedia.* 3rd edition. New York: Columbia University Press, 1963.

Carrighar, Sally. *Wild Heritage.* Boston: Houghton Mifflin, 1965.

Chayes, Abram and Wiesner, Jerome B., eds. *ABM: An Evaluation of the Decision to Deploy an Antiballistic Missile System.* New York: Harper and Row, 1969.

Clark, Harold F. and Sloan, Harold S. *Classrooms in The Military.* New York: Bureau of Publications, Teachers College, Columbia University, 1964.

Davis, Jr., James W. and Dolbeare, Kenneth M. *Little Groups of Neighbors: The Selective Service System.* Chicago: Markham Publishing Co., 1968.

Duke University Symposium Committee. *Dimensions of Defense.* Symposium held on 11 to 14 November 1962. Durham, North Carolina, 1962.

Glick, Edward Bernard. *Peaceful Conflict: The Nonmilitary Use of the Military.* Harrisburg, Pennsylvania: Stackpole Books, 1967.

Glick, Edward Bernard. *United States Navy Civic Action: Its Status and Outlook.* Ann Arbor, Michigan: Office of National Security Studies of the Bendix Corporation for the Office of Naval Research and the Naval Research Laboratory, March 1967.

Hanning, Hugh. *The Peaceful Uses of Military Forces.* New York: Frederick A. Praeger in cooperation with the World Veterans Federation, 1967.

Hays, Colonel Samuel H. *Defense Manpower: The Management of Military Conscription.* Washington, D.C.: Industrial College of the Armed Forces, 1967.

Hays, Colonel Samuel H. and Rehm, Lieutenant Colonel Thomas H., eds. *Readings in American Military Institutions and Manpower.* West Point, New York: United States Military Academy, 1968.

Heise, J. Arthur. *The Brass Factories.* Washington, D.C.: Public Affairs Press, 1969.

Huntington, Samuel P. *The Soldier and the State.* New York: Vintage Books, 1957.

Janowitz, Morris. *The Military in the Political Development of New Nations.* Chicago: University of Chicago Press, 1964.

Janowitz, Morris, ed. *The New Military: Changing Patterns of Organization.* New York: Russell Sage Foundation, 1964.

Kuslan, Louis I. and Stone, A. Harris. *Teaching Children Science: An Inquiry Approach.* Belmont, California: Wadsworth Publishing Company, Inc., 1968.

Lee, Ulysses. *United States Army in World War II: Employment of Negro Troops.* Washington, D.C.: Office of the Chief of Military History, 1966.

Lyons, Gene M. and Masland, John W. *Education and Military Leadership.* Princeton: Princeton University Press, 1959.

Masland, John W. and Radway, Laurence I. *Soldiers and Scholars.* Princeton: Princeton University Press, 1957.

Miller III, James C., ed. *Why the Draft? The Case for a Volunteer Army.* Baltimore: Penguin Books, 1968.

Nelson, Dennis D. *The Integration of the Negro into the U.S. Navy.* New York: Farrar, Straus and Young, 1951.

Nelson, William R., ed. *The Politics of Science.* New York: Oxford University Press, 1968.

Prucha, Francis Paul. Broadax and Bayonet: *The Role of the United States Army in the Building of the Northwest, 1815–1860.* Madison: State Historical Society of Wisconsin, 1953.

Puckett, Robert H. *The Military Role in Space: A Summary of Official, Public Justifications.* P–2681. Santa Monica, California: RAND Corporation, August 1962.

Radway, Laurence I. *Foreign Policy and National Defense.* Glenview, Illinois: Scott, Foresman and Co., 1969.

Reynolds, Russel B. *The Officer's Guide.* Harrisburg, Pennsylvania: Stackpole Books, 1969.

Stillman II, Richard J. *Integration of the Negro in the U.S. Armed Forces.* New York: Frederick A. Praeger, 1968.

Sulzberger, C. L. *A Long Row of Candles.* New York: Macmillan, 1969.

Swomley, Jr., John M. et al. *Militarism in Education.* Washington, D.C.: National Council Against Conscription, 1950.

Tasker, Lieutenant Frederic C. "ROTC and the University: Friends or Enemies?" Unpublished paper, n.d.

Waterhouse, Harry F. *A Time to Build.* Columbia: University of South Carolina Press, 1964.

Weigley, Russell F. *Towards an American Army.* New York: Columbia University Press, 1962.

Articles

Biderman, Albert D. "Sequels to a Military Career: The Retired Military Professional." *The New Military: Changing Patterns of Organization.* Edited by Morris Janowitz. New York: Russell Sage Foundation, 1964, pp. 287–336.

"Black Power in Vietnam." *Time* (19 September 1969), pp. 22–23.

Bradford, Donald F. "The Defense Economic Adjustment Program." *Defense Management Journal* 4 (Winter 1967–68), pp. 26–30.

"Cooperative Education Program." *Army Digest* 22 (November 1967), pp. 50–51.

"Defense Extends 'Open Housing' Ban to Pentagon Area." *Commanders Digest* 3 (30 December 1967), pp. 1, 4.

"DOD Amends Program for College Early Release." *Commanders Digest* 4 (27 January 1968), p. 4.

Driver, William J. "Your Veterans Rights and Benefits." *Army Digest* 23 (May 1968), pp. 35–38.

Engelhardt, Lieutenant Robert W. "Policing Up Recruits." *Army Digest* 24 (January 1969), pp. 41–43.

Erickson, Colonel James L. "Bringing the School to the Man." *Army Digest* 22 (November 1967), pp. 39–41.

Galbraith, John Kenneth. "The Big Defense Firms are Really Public Firms." *New York Times Magazine* (16 November 1969), p. 50.

Ginsburgh, Colonel Robert N. "The Challenge to Military Professionalism." *Foreign Affairs* 42 (January 1964), pp. 255–68.

Glick, Edward Bernard. "Alaskan Civic Action." *Military Review* 46 (December 1966), pp. 57–61.

Glick, Edward Bernard. " 'And the Builders Had Every One His Sword.' " *Jewish Frontier* 35 (March 1968), pp. 17–19.

Glick, Edward Bernard (with Major Edward J. Laurance). "Combat and Civic Action: Are They Compatible?" *Army* 17 (August 1968), pp. 71–72.

Glick, Edward Bernard. "Conflict, Civic Action and Counterinsurgency." *Orbis* 10 (Fall 1966), pp. 899–910.

Glick, Edward Bernard. "The Draft and Nonmilitary National Service." *Military Review* 49 (December 1969), pp. 86–90.

Glick, Edward Bernard. "Military Civic Action: Thorny Art of the Peace Keepers." *Army* 17 (September 1967), pp. 67–70.

Glick, Edward Bernard (with Robert Boguslaw and Robert H. Davis). "National Policy Formation in a Less Armed World." *Behavioral Science* 11 (January 1966), pp. 43–61.

Glick, Edward Bernard. "The Nonmilitary Use of the Latin American Military." *Latin America: Politics, Economics, and Hemispheric Security.* Edited by Norman A. Bailey. New York: Frederick A. Praeger for the Center for Strategic Studies of Georgetown University, 1965, pp. 179–91.

Glick, Edward Bernard. "The Nonmilitary Use of the Latin American Military: A More Realistic Approach to Arms Control and Economic Development." *Background* (Since renamed *International Studies Quarterly*) 8 (November 1964), pp. 161–73.

Glick, Edward Bernard. "On Militarism." *Congress Bi-Weekly* 36 (13 January 1969), pp. 21–22.

Glick, Edward Bernard. "ROTC: From Riot to Reason." *Air Force/Space Digest.* (October 1970), pp. 70–73.

Glick, Edward Bernard. "Scholars, Soldiers, and Society." *Air Force/Space Digest* (November 1969), pp. 59–63.

Glick, Edward Bernard. "Should We Eliminate or Merge Our Military Academies?" *Foreign Service Journal* 48 (January 1971).

Goodman, Walter. "Choose Your War; Or, The Case of the Selective C.O." *New York Times Magazine* (23 March 1969), p. 34.

Hartley, Anthony. "Antimilitarism Can Be Too Much of a Good Thing." *New York Times Magazine* (19 October 1969), p. 30.

Hersh, Seymour M. "Dare We Develop Biological Weapons?" *New York Times Magazine* (28 September 1969), p. 28.

Heymont, Colonel Irving (Ret.). "The Israeli Career Officer Corps." *Military Review* 48 (October 1968), pp. 13–19.

Huntington, Samuel P. "Interservice Competition and the Political Roles of the Armed Services." *American Political Science Review* 55 (March 1961), pp. 40–52.

Inman, Lieutenant Commander Richard P. "Computer-Assisted Education at the Naval Academy." *EDUCOM* 4 (March 1969), pp. 3–7.

Johnson, Thomas A. "Negroes in 'The Nam.' " *Ebony* 23 (August 1968), p. 31.

Kaufman, Richard F. "As Eisenhower Was Saying . . . 'We Must Guard Against Unwarranted Influence by the Military-Industrial Complex.' " *New York Times Magazine* (22 June 1969), p. 10.

Lapp, Ralph E. "The Weapons Industry is a Menace." *Saturday Evening Post* (15 June 1968), p. 10.

Lazure, Albert C. "Small Business and Labor Surplus Areas." *Defense Management Journal* 4 (Winter 1967–1968), pp. 22–25.

Leavitt, William. "Project 100,000: An Experiment in Salvaging People." *Air Force/Space Digest* (January 1968), pp. 59–64.

Little, Roger W. "Basic Education and Youth Socialization in the Armed Forces." *American Journal of Orthopsychiatry* 38 (July 1968), pp. 869–76.

Llorens, David. "Why Negroes Reenlist." *Ebony* 23 (August 1968), p. 87.

Lyons, Gene M. "The New Civil-Military Relations," *American Political Science Review* 55 (March, 1961), pp. 53–63.

McCarthy, Senator Eugene J. "The Power of the Pentagon." *Saturday Review* (21 December 1968), p. 8.

McLean, L. Deckle. "The Black Man and the Draft," *Ebony* 23 (August 1968), pp. 61–66.

McWhinter, William A. "[The National Guard:] Favorite Haven for the Comic Soldier." *Life* (27 October 1967), pp. 86–98.

Middleton, Commander W. D. "Seabees in Vietnam." *United States Naval Institute Proceedings* 93 (August 1967), pp. 55–64.

de Neufville, Richard. "Education at the Academies . . . Where Next?" *Military Review* 47 (May 1967), pp. 3–9.

Oliver, Richard P. "The Employment Effect of Defense Expenditures." *Monthly Labor Review* (September 1967), pp. 9–16.

Pilisuk, Marc. "A Reply to Roger Little: Basic Education and Youth Socialization Anywhere Else." *American Journal of Orthopsychiatry* 38 (July 1968), pp. 877–81.

Poinsett, Alex. "The Negro Officer," *Ebony* 23 (August 1968), pp. 136–41.

Pool, Ithiel de Sola. "The Necessity for Social Scientists Doing Research for Governments." *Background* (since renamed *International Studies Quarterly*) 10 (August, 1966), pp. 111–22.

Pursell, Jr., Carroll W. "Science and Government Agencies." *Science and Society in the United States*. Edited by David Van Tassel and Michael Hall. Homewood, Illinois: Dorsey Press, 1966, pp. 223–49.

Rapaport, Harold. "Technical Feasibility of War Safety Control Systems." *War Safety Control Report*. Edited by Howard G. and Harriet B. Kurtz. Chappaqua, New York: War Control Planners, 1964, pp. 21–65.

Resor, Stanley R. "Project One Hundred Thousand." *Defense Management Journal* 3 (Fall 1967), pp. 3–6.

Rutzick, Max A. "Worker Skills in Current Defense Employment." *Monthly Labor Review* (September 1967), pp. 17–20.

Sharp, Laure M. and Biderman, Albert D. "Out of Uniform." *Monthly Labor Review* (February 1967), pp. 39–47.

Walker, Lieutenant Colonel Robert M. (Ret.). "In Defense of the Military Mind." *Military Review* 49 (August 1969), pp. 55–62.

Wool, Harold. "The *Changing* Pattern of Military Skills." *Employment Security Review* (July 1963), pp. 1–6.

Young, Jr., Whitney M. "When the Negroes in Vietnam Come Home." *Harper's Magazine* (June 1967), pp. 63–69.

Zald, Mayer N. and Simon, William. "Career Opportunities and Commitments Among Officers." *The New Military: Changing Patterns of Organization.* Edited by Morris Janowitz. New York: Russell Sage Foundation, 1964, pp. 257-85.

Index